FO

Margaret Collier first came to my attention in 1989, when I heard that she had booked a local Football Stadium for an exhibition of Clairvoyance.

At the time, she had no guarantee of success but so confident was she that, following guidance from Spirit, she undertook the public demonstration and managed to fill the Stadium.

Margaret is a lady of determination who is dedicated to her work; she deserves every success.

Derek Jameson

THE GIFT IS NOT FOR ME

Margaret Collier

THE GIFT IS NOT FOR ME
A BERESFORD BOOK

ISBN 1 897644 00 0

First Publication in Great Britain

PRINTING HISTORY
Beresford Edition published 1992

Copyright © Margaret Collier, 1992

The right of Margaret Collier to be identified as author of this work has been asserted in accordance with the Copyright Designs and Patents Act 1988 Sections 77 & 78.

Conditions of sale
This book is sold subject to the condition that it shall not, by way of trade or otherwise, be lent, re-sold, hired out or otherwise circulated in any form of binding or cover other than that in which it is published and without a similar condition including this condition being imposed on the subsequent purchaser.

Published by Beresford Books, an imprint of Camtec,
1-5 Station Approach, Birchington, Kent CT7 9RD.

Typeset in 11pt Times
by Island Impressions, Birchington, Kent.

Printed and bound in Great Britain by BPCC Hazells Ltd.

PREFACE

Having produced a tape, "Psychic Development for Beginners," I had discussed with my friend Annie Hewitt the possibility of putting it into book form. We had started this but, through pressure of work, had allowed it to lapse for a few months.

Coming downstairs early one morning, I heard my foster mother, Esther, say to me, "Get your book done!" (Esther had died in 1978)

I had just reached for the telephone to suggest to Annie that we should get busy with the book, when my mother suddenly said, "No! Not *that* book. Your own life story!"

I was shocked and surprised; bursting into tears, I told her I couldn't write such a book.

"You have to," Mum said.

I just sat there, on the bottom stair, and cried.

"Don't worry, I'll help you - but you must write it for the benefit of others like yourself."

And help me she did...

This book is dedicated to Esther Hutchison.

Margaret Collier
Westgate, 1992

ONE

"Send her back." Those words were from Auntie Teenie, rather concerned that her sister had gone all the way to Glasgow Welfare Department to foster yet another child, to add to the two boys she'd already undertaken to look after.

"The boys are healthy enough, but this Margaret; she's nearly eighteen months old, covered in scabies, got tuberculosis; and first size baby dresses drown her. As if that's not enough, she's as bald as a coot. Get rid of her, Esther!"

That was the reception I got after having been abandoned by my mother when I was nine months old. She had left me with a friend who eventually delivered me to the Welfare Department in George Street in Glasgow.

My eventful past was just the beginning of a more than eventful future. I'm sure that if Esther Hutchison had been able to see into the future she would have heeded her sister's advice in the beginning and sent me back.

It has been said that people close to death gain some sort of insight. Was I that close, or was I born gifted? Only God knows. But, whichever it was, he had sent me on a mission, with one foot on this side, and one foot on the spirit side. This remains with me today, and will throughout the rest of my life.

Being psychic was much more difficult during the

war. It was not accepted, and was kept behind closed doors. More people accept and appreciate our work now, but it is with my mother's encouragement from the spirit side that I am writing this book. Without her, I could not have succeeded; in fact, I would never have even started to write it.

My mother prompted me to do it. She feels she owes it to me and to everybody else in this world, especially those who, perhaps, have psychic children and do not understand. All she wants to do is to say to you all, "Try to understand these children and encourage them, because they are gifted."

Born Margaret McGuigan on the 6th January 1942, I eventually arrived at Northglen Craig, a small mining community in the Kingdom of Fife, to continue, if I lasted my life, with Esther and Jackie Hutchison, staunch Roman Catholics.

Pat and Frank, also children from the Welfare Department, but not related, were there already. Pat is two years older than me and Frank six months. Perhaps I didn't have much life in me, but I'm told I could talk. At eighteen months, my mother said, I could talk the hind legs off a donkey, and 'all rubbish', according to her. I was forever talking to people who weren't there. This was my misfortune then and for many years to come.

Our house was in a row of pit-houses, the front facing the main street and the back looking towards the pit dross-heap, always smouldering and smelling.

Dad worked constant night shift in the pit and, every morning, we'd find him singing away in a tin bath in front of the fire, a huge open black grate, washing the filth out of his hair, eyes and body. He always looked like Al Jolson to me and would give a lovely rendition of 'Mammy', which would make me laugh and dance about.

It was during one of these bath times that I vividly remember seeing the soldier coming out of our fireplace. I was sitting on the floor next to Dad and wondered why he continued to wash away.

"There's a man Dad."

"Where?" he replied.

"Over there." By now the man had moved to the kitchen table which was in the middle of the room.

"You're imagining again, Margaret. Nobody's there."

"But he is, Dad; he's a soldier."

Mum was a couple of doors away at her sister's. "You'd better not let your mum hear you or she'll belt you for saying such things."

I was no more than four years old then, and just couldn't understand what I was going to be belted for. Of course, being the chatterbox that I was, I told Mum of our visitor as soon as she came through the door. "You'll go to Hell, lady," a name I was always called when I was in trouble. "You'd better stop telling lies or that's where you'll end up."

"Mum, he was there." The tears were already running down my face. Slap! Her hand came across my face. I don't think that the slap would have been so bad, but it was the sheer speed with which it hit my face that bothered me.

"Margaret Hutchison, get to bed this minute, you're going back to Glasgow tomorrow morning, first thing."

Totally confused and hurt, I remember lying in bed,

a recess in the wall where we all slept, thinking that Hell must be in Glasgow somewhere, wherever Glasgow was.

Next morning, there was an awful lot of upset in the house. There were my dad's brothers and sisters, and my mum's sisters, all crying. I automatically joined in as I didn't entirely know what was going on; all I did know was that I was going to Hell that day.

Feeling totally afraid, I turned and belted Frank across the face. I was always the one in trouble, so I must have done it to try to get *him* into trouble. He started screaming and Mum got hold of me, belted me hard and sent me to get my coat. Jesus, Mary and Joseph, this is it. Hell, here I come!

"Jackie, take her out of here with you...", Mum screamed, "... or I'll kill her."

My coat was shoved on me roughly, and Dad grabbed my hand and headed me out of the door. Walking down the road with him I was in hysterics, pleading with him not to take me back to Glasgow.

"You're not going to Glasgow, you're coming to Auntie Bunty's and Lochgelly with me."

Dad was crying his eyes out, too. Perhaps he doesn't want me to go, I thought. But when we got to Auntie Bunty's I soon found out why. Auntie Bunty had died after giving birth to her son James. She was in her early twenties.

I remember the long walk back from Lochgelly. Dad, myself and baby James. We kept him. I used to watch him in his pram, with the woman forever bending over him, soothing and singing to him, and, as usual, putting myself in a position to get belted for making things up.

According to Mum, I upset her so much one day, she dragged me up the road to her parish priest. "Father," said Mum, crying, "I don't know what I'm going to do with this one; I'm at the end of my tether with her. She keeps seeing all sorts of people who are not there and I can't handle her any more."

Father told me firmly, "Little girls should be seen and not heard, so we'll hear no more of this, Margaret. You're making your poor mother ill with worry, and God is none too happy with you. You don't want to end up in Hell, do you?"

Gosh, he knows about Hell as well. It must be a terrible place. I'd better shut up or that's where I'll end up.

Our chapel was a view away from the pit house, and all families who attended Mass had their own pews. We'd all shuffle in every Sunday, taking up our appointed row, and I'd sit, bored with the whole thing, watching Mum sucking on her boiled sweets before going up to the altar for communion.

Pat and Frank and I all fidgeted; we were fed up and starving. On Sundays, we had to wait for breakfast as Mum and Dad were having communion, and we were not allowed to eat beforehand. So this was why she always had sweeties in her pocket at Mass on Sundays.

It's still eating, I thought. "Mum, is it OK to eat sweets at chapel but not food?" Sad for me; when I said it, the priest was talking to her. The result was that I was thumped all the way home. What had I said? I must have been real trouble.

We had the best playground in the world at the back of our house. Coal-dust, wagons, puddles, and frogs leaping everywhere. I was forever putting tadpoles in my socks, much to Mum's horror.

"You're from the devil lady, that's it, you're not allowed to wear socks anymore. I'll swing for you one of these days."

Whatever does she mean? My wailing about the poor tadpoles and frogs freezing to death at the coal tip fell on deaf ears but, I can tell you, my ears were none too healthy for the rest of the night.

"Pat, Frank, if she goes near those frogs and tadpoles, get straight home and tell me. In fact, the bloody lot of you keep away from them. Oh, Holy Father, she's making me blaspheme."

That was it, was I unpopular! Pat thumped me as soon as we were out of sight of the kitchen window. Frank, in turn, always seemed sympathetic towards me, so he would fight with Pat, who always got the better of both of us.

Soon James was out playing with us; we were not allowed in and out of the house as Dad slept through the day. We must have got filthy dirty. Mum left us a piece of soap outside in the kitchen window-sill, with a pail of water for us to wash our faces and hands before we dared come in for our tea. Pat, being the eldest, must have had some hard times. He was always in charge, and always got me into trouble for something or other.

Exploring the tip one day, I found my secret place; I found a deep pit where the wagons carried the coal. I could climb down an iron ladder and was then totally hidden from sight; looking up, all I could see was the undercarriage of the bogey. This'll do me. My own wee secret place. Playing down there was great, and I used to talk to this man who always told me to be careful on the ladder and not to play there when it was raining. He was a nice man. He told me his name was Davy and he worked at the pit; unknown to me, Davy was on the spirit side, but I only found this out some years later.

My hideaway was soon to be discovered and I would no longer be able to spend my happy hours there with Davy and all my childish thoughts. During a terrific thunderstorm, I'd been missing for hours and, unknown to me, everyone in the pit row was out searching. Mum was the one who found me, I could hear her yelling at the top of her voice, "I know you're there, lady. Come here at once!"

Did I get the hiding of my life! Years later, Mum told me that she had been naturally drawn to my hideaway. You may realise that a pit head has many, many, dangerous places, and her first reaction on stumbling across me was a sense of relief and anger, which resulted in me being belted again. I remember today that I was never cuddled or kissed as a child but, then, the Hutchison family were not the kissing kind.

"Right you lot, up for school!" The day had dawned that Frank and I were starting school; we were both still four years old. Hand in hand, we walked behind Pat, who was an old hand and very put out at having to drag us with him. He warned me that I was not to let any of his pals know I was his sister; he had told them he only had two brothers. This lie was to continue through secondary school as well. He was, for some reason, most ashamed of me.

Mr Barnes, the Headmaster, was a balding, stout

man who took an instant dislike to me. My mother had warned him that I was more than a handful, and he was to deal with me as he saw fit. She told him not to be fooled by my Shirley Temple looks, nor by the fact that I was smaller than the rest of the class. My bald head had, by this time, transformed into a mass of beautiful curls, which were a talking-point among the neighbours.

Unlike my brothers, I was very inquisitive and wanted to know absolutely everything. I was also full of mischief. It was no secret that the Hutchison kids came from a childrens' home and Mr Barnes always pointed out this fact when, for the umpteenth time, I was sent to stand outside his door.

I was a very naive child and was always caught talking in class, and always admitted to anything I did, while the other kids denied things and put the blame on me. I was given the cat of nine tails across my hands so many times and, when I protested, Mr Barnes would shout "Double up." That was definitely torture, when you had to place the back of one hand onto the palm of the other and down came that leather belt with an almighty whack. The others used to shout, "Rub chalk on your hands." Seemingly, it didn't hurt so much, but Mr Barnes was wise to that and always sent me to wash the chalk off first, which made the pain worse as my hands were wet.

Regardless of all this, I loved school. I loved reading, writing and spelling, so I always had good reports. I was also a good singer and was always chosen to sing at school concerts; I was in the choir at Chapel and, as I grew older, I had to be there to sing at weddings. I didn't like this task very much as it meant that I couldn't play, but Mum used to say it kept me out of trouble.

I became quite holy during this time and decided, at the ripe old age of five, that I was going to sing my way to Heaven. I looked angelic, could remember all the words to the hymns and sang in tune. What more could a girl want? Besides, I knew the very place.

Mum had a cousin who had been a nun in Edinburgh since the year dot; she remained in her cell most of the time and was only allowed to talk to visitors through a grille. I remember Mum saying she even flogged herself. Well that's great, because you wouldn't hit yourself so hard, would you? Yes, that's the life for me, thank you very much. No more slaps across the back of your head that sent you flying to Kingdom Come. No more weals across your wrist when the headmaster deliberately missed the palm of your hand. Yes, Heaven, here I come.

Sundays always found us permitted to sit in our front parlour, the only room that had a view of the main street, and the only day, except for special occasions, when we could go out of the house through the front door. We'd all sift out in our Sunday best, remembering, too, that we were clad better than the families around us.

Our benefactor, except for James, was the Welfare Department who paid for our clothes, and Mum had found a God-fearing woman in Glenrothes, a good Catholic, who could do anything with a needle. She made my dresses and coats, and how I hated that woman. She made me stand like a statue for ages while she measured me and pinned the material draped over me, pulling me this way and then that way.

"Stand still Margaret," she'd say. God, if I'd stood still much longer, rigor mortis would have set in. She was the most dour woman, was always at Mass, never smiled, and exchanged all the gossip with my mum. They would blather about everybody over a pot of tea and a piece of Mum's home-made cake which, I was reminded, was not made for me, so I was to say 'No' if I was offered a slice.

Mum always made a cake to take to the dressmaker because she'd had a hard life, poor woman, and was struggling to make ends meet, Mum said. Her man had left her some years before. I'm not surprised, I thought, who would want to live with her anyway? I couldn't stomach her for an hour, never mind live with her. Mum's cakes were the talk of the neighbourhood but, as I have said, we were forewarned not to touch, but could have what our visitors left.

One Sunday, I was playing on the floor while Mum was getting James dressed in the kitchen, when I saw a lady just standing there, looking at me. She scared me because she wouldn't speak; I said 'Hello,' and she just stared. I flew into the kitchen crying, "Mum there's a lady in the sitting-room."

My mother was not amused. "How many times have I told you not to come in here when you're dressed up?" Sundays, after she had dressed us, we were sent straight into the parlour, so we had no chance of getting ourselves dirty. We all argued to be dressed last; it gave us some extra playing time. I was always dressed first. "Now, stop your silly stories, you'll be the death of me, lady." She then proceeded to preach the unpardonable sin. She never did define the unpardonable sin, but never failed to make me feel that I had committed it.

Back I went to the parlour. What a relief, the lady was no longer there. Perhaps Mum had scared her; I hoped so, anyway. So, out we set for Mass, clean as new pins, with me smelling to high heaven of cold cream rubbed into my face and my lacy hankie, sprayed with Mum's perfume, stuck up my sleeve. I wasn't allowed to use my hankie; it was only for show. If I wanted to blow my nose, Mum kept an old rag in her pocket, beside her boiled sweeties.

Once again we went through the rigmarole, the congregation lustily singing of Heaven and the priest preaching of Hell and Damnation. What else could he save us from if not Hell and Protestants? And not necessarily in that order!

I saw the lady a few times after that, each time in the parlour. She wore a long, dark dress and a shawl covered her shoulders. A shiny brooch held the shawl together. I would always make an excuse to Mum that I needed the toilet, so as not to be on the receiving end of that famous hand. I had learned to lie to save the truth from getting me into trouble.

Dad never interfered with Mum; he used to say, laughingly, "There's only one boss in this house, that's your mum." We loved Dad dearly, as he was always fair with us. I especially liked it when Mum went out, because then I could tell Dad about my unseen friends and he wouldn't yell or belt me, but would just nod his head. I never felt threatened by him. He would sit down with the socks and darn; he was so neat that you'd never know where the wool had been.

Dad also loved fishing; that was his main hobby. He was a good cook, too, and his tatty scones were the best for miles around. When he wasn't down the pit head, he'd go off fishing and we would be excited to see what he'd caught when he came home.

The routine was always the same. The first fish was our doctor's, then the worst off family in our pit row would be next, then relatives. Dad would carefully dress the fish ready for cooking and, when the salmon season was in, he would carefully cut the fish up, cook it and jar the roe, dating it. Then he'd pass it around, Doctor Stevens first, then on down the line.

When the strawberries and raspberries were out, we'd find Dad arriving home with bags full on the back of his motor-bike, and then he'd make his jam, which was delicious. This also went round the town in the same way as the fish.

Dad had been a Protestant when he had first met Mum, but had converted in order to marry her. It turned out that he would be the better Catholic, as was proved later on, just as the lady I saw in the parlour was to change Mum's whole attitude towards the spirit side and myself. Unfortunately for me, this was still many years away.

I believe that I was born with this gift from God and was sent deliberately to Esther Hutchison to help us evolve each other's souls. How can someone who never suffers be able to sympathise with a sufferer? How can a poor soul feeling totally rejected turn to someone who has never felt rejection? I was being taught the only way known. Didn't He say, 'Suffer little children to come unto me'? He taught me well, and now I teach others and will continue to do so while I remain on this plane of existence.

My life is dedicated to His work and to proving there is life after death.

TWO

Frank came running outside. "We're moving."
"Moving where?" I asked.
"We've got a new house."
So it was we moved three miles up the road to a new housing estate. There were two streets already built and one family had settled in; we were the second. I couldn't take you round today, it is so big.

Our council-house contained three bedrooms, bathroom, kitchen and sitting-room. It was great. No more bits of soap nor the pail of water outside. No more tin baths on Saturday night. We were living in luxury. The front door had a nice porch, and we also had a garden, back and front and down the side because the house was semi-detached; everyone was kept busy helping in the garden. We were at the bottom of a lovely hill. No coal-dust, just fresh air and miles and miles of fields and trees to play in. The only hazard was that we had much further to go to school; buses didn't go that far uphill. There were no roads, so we had to tramp over dirt tracks and muddy fields where building was in progress.

The cemetery, which catered mainly for the mining community, was seen from the top stair window and the kirkyard was across from the sitting-room window. Perhaps society was suppressing my psychic awareness, as all was quiet on the home front for a few years. Families moved in all the time, both Catholics and Protestants. I guess the Council didn't take part in segregation of the sects, but the community certainly did. We were warned not to play with the Proddies, as they were called, and they were not allowed to play with us.

I didn't understand it then and I don't understand it now. After all, we're all 'Jock Tamson's bairns'. We were being taught to love thy neighbour, but it wasn't mentioned that they had to be Catholic. Across the street from our school was the Protestant school. They were to stay on their side and we on ours; heaven help you if you got caught talking with each other! Of course, this kind of indoctrination caused everyone to be nasty to each other; we had been baptised so, whatever our beginnings, we were now Catholics and we didn't talk to Protestants.

A gentleman from the Welfare would show up periodically to see how we kids were getting on. Mum always threatened me that he would take me back to Glasgow if I even spoke; needless to say, I was very quiet during his visits. She never threatened Pat or Frank. Mind you, Pat was always the favourite, and he seldom missed an opportunity to give us a hard time when Mum and Dad were out.

Mum used to sit and determine what sort of mothers we had started out with. The Welfare had never given out information about charges. Pat had what Mum reckoned was a 'Baw head', square in shape. His poor mother must have been raped by a German, Mum said; this, in her estimation, was why Pat was so clever at school.

After all, the German race were very clever. Frank's mum, she said, had been a nurse; this was the only fact she had ever found out. So his dad was probably a distinguished doctor. My mother must have been a prostitute, and couldn't look after me because she was so busy with all the sailors.

When I strongly protested in my unknown mother's defence, Mum would say, "Well, when you first came here in such a state, you thought the sauce bottle on the table was a bottle of beer, and the first time you set eyes on a sailor you knew he was one. So, I think she must have hung around pubs to pick up sailors."

"Maybe she was a film star," I would say. "Maybe Margaret Lockwood's my secret mum."

"Don't be daft, now stop arguing with me."

This argument, thrown at me from time to time, would always send me dreaming that one day I'd find my real mum, just to show Esther Hutchison she was wrong.

I was most offended.

It was time for Pat to sit his eleven-plus and he was given all the encouragement possible. Dad was emphatic that none of his boys was going down the pit; he himself had been down there since he the age of fourteen and he hated it, but had no choice. Pat was the poorly one; he'd had pleurisy and was cosseted because of this. Frank's health problem was a perforated eardrum, which had left him very deaf. Me, I was never sick. Dad always said it must have been the cod-liver oil I drank; I used to drink everybody's share. The only health problem I recall having was a badly sprained ankle, for which I got no sympathy. I still had to carry out my daily chores.

We were all allocated jobs, which we had to do before we went to school and when we got back in the afternoon. Pat was relieved of his duties when he was studying. He passed his eleven-plus without any difficulty, so he would be moving up to secondary school in Cowdenbeath. Frank was next, and also got through. My parents were delighted! Mum reckoned that it wasn't important for me; I was a girl so I would eventually have a good Catholic husband to support me and whatever kids we might have. Anyone who failed their eleven-plus was sent to a school in Lochgelly run by nuns. Everyone called it the daft school – you could only be daft if you went there. Mum had resigned herself to the fact that this was where I'd be going, as I wasn't half as clever as the boys. Her mind was made up about that.

"I don't believe it," Mum said. "She's only passed her eleven-plus! She must have cheated."

That was the reaction after I had proudly run all the way home to tell her the news. I think that was the day I decided that Esther Hutchison, foster-mother, didn't like me and never would. I withdrew to my bedroom, which I shared with James, who was three years younger than me, and decided I was going to commit suicide.

"Don't be stupid," James said.

"It's all right for you, James; you're the baby and she loves you."

They had legally adopted James, while we other three would have to remain under the care of the Welfare until the age of eighteen, when they would be obliged to give us any information they had on us. I couldn't wait. It didn't matter now, anyway; I was going to kill myself, just to get my own back.

"Margaret, get down these stairs and get your hair

washed this minute," Mum yelled.

"No! I'm going to drown myself, then you'll be rid of me."

"You'll have your damn hair washed first, lady. If you're going to meet your maker, he's not going to blame me for your hair being filthy."

She doesn't care one bit whether I live or die, I thought. All she cares about is my hair being clean. As I descended the stairs, feeling totally alone, I wished I'd never passed that exam.

"Now I've got to spend a fortune on a new uniform for you," she was muttering as I went into the kitchen.

"Well," I said, "you had to spend it on Pat and Frank."

"I know, but I'd made my mind up you were going to St Patrick's, and you can wear anything there."

"All right," I screamed, "I'll go to St Patrick's, just to save you a few bob." Quickly adding, "The money comes from the Welfare anyway."

Bang! I went flying across the kitchen.

"Don't you dare say that lady. I work my fingers to the bone on the pittance they give me to pay for you lot."

"Well, send me back." I was surprised to hear myself saying that, as that had always been my greatest fear.

"Mark my words, lady, I'll do just that one of these days." How true those words were to be.

So it was I boarded the school bus to begin my first day at St Columbus High School in Cowdenbeath. There was great excitement on board. As we passed by St Patrick's, everyone was banging on the bus window and yelling to those who had failed their exams. How I wish I'd been joining them; Mum would have been happier. "Don't worry Margaret," a voice whispered, "we'll look after you." I began to feel better with that bit of reassurance. My spirit friends had always treated me with kindness.

The school was vast, compared to our primary school, with so many classes to attend. I slotted in and got down to work, and found I enjoyed it very much. I loved all of my subjects, and it helped that our history teacher was a cousin of the family. The Headmaster liked me, too, so I settled in well, particularly enjoying music and art.

Mrs Jackson was a lovely soul; she was a friend of Mum's and would visit us every Tuesday. She always brought us sweeties, was kind and treated me well. I couldn't understand how Mum had got to be friends with Mrs Jackson, who was not a Catholic.

Of course, Mum had become friendly with some of her Protestant neighbours; but Mrs Jackson, she came all the way from Lochgelly, which was about fifteen minutes away, and she was a Spiritualist, whatever that meant. We all looked forward to her visits every Tuesday and watched for her walking up the street. I believe the sweets were an important part of her being welcome.

"Can I come to your house?" I asked her one day.

"Of course you can." So I got excited.

"Have you got any kids?"

"I've one daughter, but she's married, so there's only me and Uncle Tom."

So it was arranged that I was to stay the weekend with Mrs Jackson. Her little house was neat and tidy.

Uncle Tom was a very nice man and I felt safe there; I was spoken to like an adult. I settled down in bed that night feeling quite content and happy. Perhaps things were getting better now, I thought as I drifted off to sleep.

Mum hadn't seemed to have been at me so much. James had been made captain of the school football team and they had won the cup that year for the first time. Football played a big part in our family; we'd got a TV set, so the house was always full of neighbours who didn't have one, and football was the main topic of conversation. James would be running round the hills by 6 o'clock every morning. He lived, ate and slept football. Hibs was his team, and he was going to be a famous footballer one day.

I woke up suddenly and saw a man standing by the bed. "Hello Margaret," he said. "Don't mind me, I live here."

Funny, I hadn't seen him earlier on. Oh, well. I went back to sleep. Next morning, at breakfast, Mrs Jackson asked me if I'd like to visit Church with her. Not really wanting to, but wishing not to offend, I said I didn't mind. So, early that evening found Mrs Jackson and Tom and myself in church. This was a funny looking church. No pews, statues or altar; just a group of people, all chatting. I must have looked puzzled.

"Sit next to me," Mrs Jackson said. I was attending my first Spiritualist meeting. As the woman was speaking, I caught sight of the man I had seen at Mrs Jackson's house.

"I have a gentleman here, dear," the woman said, looking at Mrs Jackson. "He says to tell you the student is doing fine. Do you understand?"

"Perfectly," was the reply.

I was looking at the man who was looking at Mrs Jackson, and wondered why this woman on the stage was telling her what he said. Couldn't she hear him herself? At the end of the meeting we had a cup of tea and everybody was excitedly stood talking about the messages. I couldn't see the man anywhere, so I asked if the man who spoke to Mrs Jackson had got bored and gone home.

"What man, hen?" (A term of endearment like 'duck' or 'love', used in Scotland.)

"The man who lives at your house."

"Only Uncle Tom lives at our house."

"No, the man who was telling you about his student. I saw him last night when I was in bed."

"Well, hen, we'll talk about that when we get home."

After supper, we were sitting drinking our cocoa, and Mrs Jackson gently told me that she had known for some time that I had been given a special gift, and that the people I had been seeing since I was little were really there. But it was very difficult, she said, and it was not always the wise thing to speak about it.

"There will come a day, Margaret, when people will be queuing to see you. Always use your gift wisely and never disbelieve what the spirits tell you."

I sat in awe as she explained to me about the Spirit World. I hugged her before going to bed. She believed me, and I went home happy as a sandboy. I'd been taught a lesson, that weekend, and felt so good about it. And, because Mrs Jackson reckoned it wouldn't be wise to say too much to my mum, I kept it all to myself.

At school, a group of us girls had got together and would go down town at lunchtimes. We would go into Woolworth's and a nicking spree would begin. We'd arrive back at school with rubbers, notebooks and pencils, a fine selection. We were all guilty. We knew it was wrong but, sadly, we did it just the same. One of the girls even got a new pair of shoes.

We had just moved into our second year when the bombshell dropped; six of us were given letters to take home. We were warned not to open them. Not at all concerned, I handed mine to Mother but, on reading it, she went berserk. Picking up the poker from the fireplace, she set about me.

The screaming woke Dad. He had to run downstairs and restrain Mum, while I ran upstairs whimpering like a wounded animal. Mum was screaming, "She's a thief, a common bloody thief." Then, upstairs she came, yelling abuse at me, "You're going back, you good-for-nothing bastard."

I must have been in a state of shock, for I was shaking from head to toe. Weals were rising on my legs and arms, and I couldn't feel my back. I was warned to stay put. Crawling under the bedclothes, I was beside myself. Someone must have seen us nicking from Woolworth's, and now we were for it.

Next morning, my best friend Rachel, who lived up the street, called for me. I was still in bed.

"She's not going today," I heard Mum snap, slamming the front door.

I couldn't go; I was black and blue and could hardly move. Rachel had been given a letter, too. Her family were very close and I spent most of my time with her at their house. You could mess the place up and her mum took it all in her stride. They were a happy bunch. I used to confide in Rachel's mum; she didn't like my mum for the way she treated me and would cross the street before she would speak to her. Sadly, most of the neighbours followed suit over the next few years, as did some of Mum's relatives.

The following week found the six of us, with our mums, in the deputy-head's office. All the letter had stated was that a theft had been committed and we'd been seen in the area. Everyone was nervous. One of the girls was my cousin, my dad's sister's daughter.

The deputy-head began talking to our mums, telling them that a school scarf and some money had gone from one of the pupils' jackets hanging in the cloakroom, and it had to be one of us as we'd been larking around. We should not have been in the cloakroom, and we knew it. He wanted to know which one of us did it, or we'd all be punished severely.

We knew none of us had done it. We weren't angels, but we knew none of us was guilty of this, as it would have been mentioned. We were so relieved that Woolworth's was not the reason and, of course, we denied any knowledge of this particular theft. It was my first time back in school since my hiding; all the other girls had continued to attend as usual.

Auntie Georgina was the first to speak. "Is this what you called us all here for?" followed by murmurings from the other parents, all except my mum.

Rachel's mum said, "If she says she didn't do it, then I believe her," followed by similar retorts from the rest of the mothers.

Mum declared, "Well, I'm not covering up for Margaret, I'll not have a thief in my family. I'd be ashamed to show my face in the street."

I started crying. Here I was in a predicament, the

only one to be shown up. Not for the first time, or the last, was I to feel that I had committed the deed.

"You might as well expel this one because she's not setting foot in this school again; I've got two sons here to think about."

I cried all the way home, very uncertain about my future. The atmosphere was terrible. I was branded. My brothers were warned that they would face the same fate if they ever thought of doing such a thing. I was not allowed out; I'd just sit at the window watching my pals playing, laughing and having fun. Was I the Devil's own, as she'd said? Perhaps I was.

A few days later, while Mum was out, Rachel was walking home from school and I banged on the window and beckoned her to the front door. "What happened at school?"

"We all got a lecture and were warned we would be expelled if we were caught in the cloakroom again. When will you be back?" she said.

"I don't know if I will."

"You coming up to play later?"

"I'm not allowed out; I've got the ironing to do as well."

"Well, ask your mum if you cannot get out for a little while."

"OK. I'd better go, Dad's coming downstairs," and I quietly shut the door.

"All right. You can play for half an hour after you've washed the dishes, but keep away from Rachel McDermott's house."

I walked round the block the other way and went to Rachel's. Her mum was very upset for me. "She's a wicked woman, your mum, and God will punish her for this. She needs to be reported to the authorities for what she's doing to you," and she burst out crying. "I always say blood is thicker than water; she should have shut her mouth instead of putting the blame on you in front of the deputy headmaster."

I had to get back; my time was up, in more ways than one.

"Get your bath."

I quickly escaped into the bathroom before she could question me about where I'd been. I couldn't handle another hiding.

Next morning, she woke up James and me; putting some clothes on my bed, she told me to get dressed and told James to get ready for school.

"What do I have to get dressed for, Mum?" I said, as the clothes were not my uniform and I definitely wasn't going to school, anyway. I began to shake.

"Just shut up and do as you're told. I've had enough of you." And off she went downstairs. I was panicking as I got dressed. The clothes were new, my mind was in a tiz.

"James, you'll be late for school, get moving," she yelled.

James didn't have to be told twice, he was off. Dad was sitting staring into the fire.

"What's wrong Dad?"

"Sit down Margaret," he said. "Your mum's never been so upset and she feels she can't do any more with you. You've had chance after chance, but still you bring worry to the door."

"But Dad, I haven't done anything."

Mum walked quietly in from the kitchen. "Don't sit there telling us you've done nothing, Margaret. I can't sleep at night, wondering what you're going to do next."

I said, "But I didn't take the scarf and the money, honest. I did take the stuff from Woolworth's, but I never stole from school."

"See what I mean? You're a thief and you're also a liar. You never told us you stole from Woolworth's."

"I'll never do it again, I promise I'll be good. I'll do everything I'm told."

"You're too late to try and make amends; the Welfare are picking you up at 11 o'clock. You're going back to Glasgow."

"Dad, please don't send me away," I pleaded. "Please, I'll do anything. I'm sorry I've been nothing but trouble. I'll make you proud of me."

But all of my pleading fell on deaf ears. I flew out of the house, Mum after me, screaming my head off. She caught me and dragged me back to the house.

The big fancy car arrived, with a chauffeur and a woman who came in for me. I had only what I was dressed in; Mum had been told I wouldn't need anything else.

I was still crying when we arrived in Glasgow; Mary Hill was the place, and the car drew up at a big, elegant-looking house.

"Try not to worry," the woman said, "you'll be all right. Shall we get you something to eat?"

"No thanks." I'd had nothing, but felt I would be sick if I attempted to swallow anything.

We were greeted at the door by a nun, a Sister of Charity. She looked me up and down, said hello, and led me upstairs, after saying goodbye to the woman from the Welfare. Her long black flowing habit and her white head-dress reminded me of a sea gull.

"You'll only be here for a few days, Margaret, until your Welfare Officer sorts something out." She opened a door to reveal a huge dormitory, partitioned to make the rooms private. "This will be your bed."

It was a white painted iron frame with a mattress, the same as you see in prisons. There was a chest of drawers in the corner of the cubicle. Once again, I started to cry. I didn't think I had any more tears left; my face was swollen and my eyes were nearly closed.

"Now, come downstairs and we'll get you some dinner."

I was so tired, but I followed her down. The dining-room was sparse, with four square tables and chairs. There were two girls, who just looked up at me and carried on talking. They were older than me.

"What you here for?" one said.

"Stealing. But I didn't do it."

"Yea, we all say that, kid, don't worry about it."

However, I managed to eat something, then went upstairs and lay on my bed. I'd never felt so sad and hopeless.

At 6 am, I was wakened by one of the girls, who said we had to get down to Mass. The nuns were singing and I just helplessly watched the procedure.

I had been there three weeks when my Welfare Officer arrived. "Good morning, Margaret, we'll get you settled today," he said. "So, if you're ready, we'll get going."

I still wore the same clothes that I'd had when I arrived there. I had washed my knickers out every night but they had usually still been damp when I put them on the following morning, just like they were this morning. I didn't dare ask where I was going, so I just followed him; he was a nice, pleasant man and chatted away to me throughout the journey.

We eventually arrived in a place called Gourock, and he told me we were taking a boat trip. "You'll be fine, you're going to a home for children. It's in Dunoon and you'll be well looked after there." It was the first time I'd been on a boat.

I quickly settled down in the children's home. They were a happy bunch. The house was a long, single storey house with a large garden, with swings to play on. I suddenly began to feel better. Matron was very nice.

There were fifteen of us, all told, and dogs and cats as well. We'd had a cat at home, once, but Mum had rubbed its nose in its own dirt to teach it not to go indoors. It ran away and never came back. A very wise cat.

"Right, Margaret. Mary will take you to school with her in the morning." So, I was all kitted out in a school uniform and arrived for my first day at Dunoon Grammar School. I wasn't quite thirteen. If I had thought St Columbus was big, this was even bigger, and there were both Catholics and Protestants.

Entering the Head's study, Mary announced, "This is the new girl, Sir." The Head smiled, pleasantly.

Mary had been in the home for just over a year. Her father had been abusing her. "What did you get sent here for?" she asked.

"Mum'd had enough of me," I answered.

I settled into school and loved every minute of it. We all looked after each other and were seldom told off. Our House Mothers lived locally, so we could visit them and their families any time we liked. We were one big happy family. Rules were very few: the main one was that we were always to be dressed the same.

At school, therefore, everyone knew we were from the Home and, outside, kids and adults alike would say, "Oh, you're from the Childrens' Home." That was fine; I can't recall anyone hitting me or yelling at me all the time I was there.

Little Ronnie was my favourite. He seemed a sad little soul the day he arrived with his sister, Emma. Their dad had murdered their mum, so they didn't have a home. The poor, wee soul kept on crying; he missed his mum so much. He was only four years old but, needless to say, within a week he was a normal child again. Well, he now had a lot of brothers and sisters who looked after him and loved him.

Emma was a born mother. She was only six, and a lovely wee thing. She really had been through an awful time, and any self-pity I had for myself soon went out of the window. Here were kids who, to my mind, had suffered much more than I ever could. Those years spent at the home were the happiest of my life, and I thank God for allowing me them.

Letters were few and far between. Dad and Mrs Jackson were the only two people I ever heard from, and they occasionally put a postal order in for two and sixpence. My dad had had a bad accident on his motor-bike, so had been unable to work for over a year. Mum was fine. James still lived and breathed football. Pat and Frank were OK, too.

I would read my letters to the other kids, as most of them didn't receive any. Then, off we'd go down to the shop to change my postal order, and we'd share the sweets. Each Saturday we were given a shilling pocket money. We were fortunate children.

Now in my final year, I had grown some. My blue-black hair long and shiny, my blue eyes always full of laughter. I was the lead singer in our school band, all of whom were older than me. It was the time of Frankie Lane, Johnnie Ray, Pat Boone and Bill Hayley. I felt really grown-up singing with these fifth-year boys, and was allowed to travel with the band; we played and sang at parties, old folks homes and homes for the handicapped. It was lovely to watch those less fortunate enjoying themselves so much.

I had won an award of merit at school that year, in the Children's National Handwriting competition, and everyone at school and the home were so proud of me. I had decided to stay on at school; I wanted to study more English, Art and Music, and become a teacher myself. I was so full of plans for the future.

Sitting one night with Matron, while the others were asleep, I told her of my dreams. "Margaret, we're not allowed to have you once you've reached the age of fifteen."

"What can I do then?"

"Have a word with your Welfare Officer when he visits you next, and see what he says."

He was a nice man, married with a family of his own.

"Yes, that's what I'll do, I'm sure he'll be able to find a way."

THREE

Christmas 1956 was approaching fast; I was officially due to leave both school and the home then, as my birthday fell on the 6th of January, which was during the holidays. My Welfare Officer would be visiting me during the week before Christmas.

Great excitement flooded the place as we all got the house ready for Christmas. The decorations, the tree, and all the presents to put under it. Some of the kids would be having their first real Christmas; Santa always visited us, and we'd be going to the pantomimes and parties.

"I don't want to leave," I cried.

"I'm sorry, love, but you have to. You know you can't stay on, you're too old."

They were sending me back to Esther Hutchison. Dad was making a very slow recovery from his accident, and they had found a spot on his lung for which he was having to have an operation. Finances were none too great, and I was now, at fifteen, in a position to help out by getting a job. I had no choice; I belonged to the Glasgow Welfare Department until I was eighteen at least.

I was so sad to leave my beloved Dunoon. I left as I had arrived, in a chauffeur-driven car. I was so scared at not knowing what was ahead of me, a very unhappy young lady indeed. Matron's words echoed in my ears.

"Make the best of the situation Margaret, help all you can, and don't answer her back; it will make life easier for yourself. You can leave them when you're eighteen, if things don't work out."

Nothing much had changed at home. We'd all got taller. Dad was hobbling round on a stick; he'd had a bad time, bless him, but remained as cheerful as he possibly could, under the circumstances. Everyone was pleased to see me. Funnily enough, including Mum.

James was doing well at his football. It seemed the school team had been unbeatable since he had become captain. He was always laughing and joking, and was the apple of Mum's eye.

Pat had a good job at Rosyth Dockyard and had applied to go into the Merchant Navy on the cruise-ships. Frank was to start an apprenticeship as a Mechanical Engineer for the National Coal Board so, for the next three years, he would be earning merely a pittance.

Any talk of myself re-entering school was just not on. Pat would be leaving home if he got the job in the Merchant Navy, so there would be no 'keep' money. Frank couldn't afford much, as his books and tools had to be paid for. So I needed to earn the best money I could to supplement Dad's sick money.

"Should I apply to one of the factories in Dunfermline, Mum?"

"I'm not having you in a factory," she said. "I'll break your legs first. They're needing staff at the Co-op, so you can apply to sit their exam."

Mum was a very proud person and would rather go with the few bob less that I would earn at the Co-op, than the extra I would get working at the factory.

I sat, and passed, the exam. To be honest, I had considered deliberately failing it; I wanted to go to the factory because all my old friends were there.

At the Co-op, they all knew that I had been taken away, so I knew I was going to have to face some smart jibes. However, I settled down into the job and quite enjoyed it. Rachel and I spent many happy evenings doing each other's hair, making up, and learning to rock and roll.

We would attend the local dance hall on Friday nights. I was earning two pounds ten shillings a week; Mum had two pounds keep, my fares were five shillings, and five shillings went in my pocket. Mum gave me a few cigarettes every day and bought my clothes, so I didn't want for anything. She was obviously feeling easier about my spirit friends, as she would talk more openly in my presence. However, I was very wary about saying anything; I had learned to keep quiet.

One evening, Rachel and I were sat trying not to laugh, as our face-packs were setting and, as we girls knew, a giggle would just crack the whole thing; you ended up with lines all over your face, like a roadmap or, worse, something from a horror picture.

Mum arrived home with a few of my Aunties. They were buzzing about something; Auntie Peg was the first to speak.

"You're going to be a famous singer," she said.

"Am I?" I replied, wondering if she'd had a few too many to drink at the club.

"She said you're going to be famous for your voice."

"Who did?"

"We went to an old fortune-teller, and she was very good."

Then Mum said, "Your dad's getting better, James will end up playing for Scotland, and things are going to be all right."

Thank God for that, I thought, feeling much more secure about my future life after such a revelation.

When Mrs Jackson paid her usual visit, Mum told her all about it.

"You mustn't believe everything a fortune-teller tells you, Esther."

"I'm inclined to believe what she said because she seemed to know so much," Mum replied.

"She's an old soul, that one, she's been here before."

This made me tremble a bit, as I remembered that, when I had been little, she used to say that about me. I shrugged it off.

"Plus, that healer we went to see in London said he would send absent healing on Jackie..."

My mum went to a healer? With her, it was always at Mass.

"... and he does seem better," she added.

It turned out that Mrs Jackson and Mum had been to see a healing demonstration when they had visited Aunty Anne in London while I'd been away. The healer was a man called Harry Edwards.

Mrs Jackson, seeing the opening, replied, "Margaret, he's a great healer, a worker for God. He helps so many people who are sick. He's one of God's right-hand men down here."

"But Mum, you don't believe in anything like that!"

"Listen," she said, "I saw with my own eyes what

that man did for people. They were throwing their sticks away. The atmosphere couldn't have been more spiritual if I'd been walking through the pearly gates to meet my maker; I'll never forget that night for the rest of my life. It was a miracle, that's all I can say about it."

Well, I thought to myself, she's definitely made up her mind. Mrs Jackson smiled knowingly at me.

I'd been at the Co-op nearly three months and all seemed well, when James kept me up all through one night with a terrible toothache. We still shared a room. Mum kept him off school and took him to the dentist to have the tooth removed. Now, no one likes the dentist and James was no exception.

A few days later found him still poorly; as we lay in our beds, he complained about feeling cold. I said, "Come in beside me, I'll keep you warm."

He slid under the blankets beside me and I cuddled him up close. His feet and legs were like marble. I rubbed and rubbed but they didn't get warm.

"Margaret," he said, "I think I'm going to die."

"Don't be stupid James, of course you're not." We chatted away.

"If I do, I'll come back and tell you if I'm all right."

"Stop talking like that, you're not going anywhere, you're going to play for Scotland, so no more of that daft talk."

The next morning found James shivering in front of the fire. I had stayed home because he wanted me beside him, and Mum had agreed. All of a sudden, Mum shouted at me to get the doctor; she could see James' knees swelling up as he sat beside me. I ran next door to our neighbours; the Maguires had all boys who were haemophiliacs, so a telephone had been installed as a necessity.

The doctor came straight away, and James was taken to the Sick Childrens' Hospital in Edinburgh. A few days after being admitted, he became blind. The family managed to contact Hibs footballer Laurie Riley, hoping that, if his hero visited him, James would make a quick recovery. Kindly, Laurie did visit him, but to no avail.

The following day, Friday, April the 19th, 1957, James was dead. He was eleven years old, and had never had a day's illness during his short life. Nephritis was the cause, they said.

Mum, Dad, and all the family were inconsolable. His little body was brought home on Saturday night and put in the sitting-room. The priest said Mass in front of his open coffin, in our front room at midnight.

Watching everybody's faces, I realised that none of them could see James standing with his arms around my mum. I looked from him standing there, into the coffin, and could see the body lying there. Tears were streaming down my face, as they were down everyone else's.

When I eventually got to bed, I could feel him getting in with me.

"I'm all right, Margaret," he whispered.

Oh, God! How can I even mention this?

It was Easter Sunday. Mum was beside herself and, at one point, had even taken James out of the coffin. He was buried on Easter Monday with the whole school in attendance. Pat had locked himself in his room, and hadn't spoken to anyone. We'd all taken it very badly.

A week later, Dad told me I was to go with Mum to Aunty Anne's in London for a week, so that Mum could rest a bit.

Aunty Anne was a lady, always so smart. Queenly, I always thought. She held a long cigarette holder when she smoked. She was elegance itself. Never a hair out of place, 'neat' was a word meant for her. She was my mother's only brother's fourth wife, and I could never imagine what she could possibly see in Uncle Matt. He was fat and bald, but generous to a fault. Always kind to us kids.

They lived in a flat in Paddington. Outside, above the door downstairs, I spotted the bust of a man. What a funny place to put an ornament, I thought. Aunty Anne, seeing me ponder over it, told me it was a lady's spirit guide.

"Spirit guide?"

"Yes, the lady's a spiritualist medium but, if she bothers you, just tell her you're a Catholic and she'll leave you alone. She was found buried alive during the blitz; everyone with her was dead. That must have affected her; she talks to unseen people all the time, poor woman. She really should be locked up."

On our way out, a few days later, the medium was standing at her door.

"Why don't you come in for a cuppa and a chat?" she said to Mum.

"No thank you, we're just off out."

As we walked away, the lady called to Mum, "Your boy's fine, love."

We both stopped in our tracks. "What boy?"

"Your son, my love. He's there beside you."

I burst out crying.

"Shut up, Margaret."

With that, Mum turned and walked back to her. "I will have that cuppa, if it's still on offer."

"You are most welcome," she said.

Mum told me to sit on the stairs outside and wait for her, but the lady said, "No, please, let her come in, she has already seen him — haven't you, love?"

"Yes," I croaked.

Shaking like a leaf, I followed behind Mum into the medium's flat. She was a kindly-looking soul, and her flat was neat and tidy. Making small conversation, she brought us tea.

"I know you may find it difficult to believe, love, but your son wants you to stop fretting and pull yourself together."

Mum replied, "I've seen him too." Tears welling up in her eyes. "It was the night he was brought home from the hospital. I had gone past sleep and was just lying in bed, when he walked towards me, like he was coming through the curtains, and then he asked me for a drink. He was sick; you see, he was not allowed anything to drink and he was so thirsty. I got up and went downstairs, and brought him a cup of milk. 'Here you are, son,' I said to him and he smiled, said, 'Thanks Mum,' and just disappeared."

"Yes, love, he craved that drink and he came to you because he knew he'd get one," she went on, "That was all the satisfaction he needed, he didn't really have to drink it."

I was really shaken. That had been the night James had got into bed with me. Mum had seen him, too!

"You must try to understand, love," the medium said as they chatted on. "You may sit and watch a television set or talk on the phone, but not understand how they work, but it's good to know there is someone at the shop you can turn to for help if there is a problem. It's the same when someone dies; it's sensible to call for somebody who understands, who has knowledge. Not everyone knows how to fix a TV or a phone, just as not everyone understands what happens after death."

She was a very wise woman. She turned to me and said, "And you, my love, never, ever deny the spirit side; you are here for a purpose, to benefit mankind. You are being taught and your spirit guide will be made known to you as time goes by. Jesus was denied, wasn't he? He didn't pass his power only to his Apostles, dear, so always use it wisely. He has given it to you."

We felt so much better for meeting that lovely soul. She was one of many to impress me over the next thirty years.

FOUR

After arriving back in Fife, Mum seemed to go down-hill again. There is nothing worse on this earth than to lose a child, and she sank lower and lower, further into depression each day. Anger took over, and we all tried to keep out of her way.

She flew at me one day and started blaming me for James' death, screaming that it should have been me instead. It seemed I had turned her away from God with my talk of spirits, and he had punished her by taking away the one thing she loved. It was terrible. I then told her how I hated her so much, how she'd always blamed me for everything and that I'd be glad to get away from her for good.

A few days later, Dad came into my room and told me to get up. It was an hour before I usually got up for work, so I knew something was up. I went downstairs to find Dad sobbing his heart out. Mum had been onto the Welfare and had told them to get me out of her house. I easily resigned myself to this, as I no longer wanted to remain. I packed my clothes and waited for the car. I couldn't take any more, either.

Because there hadn't been time for my Welfare Officer to arrange a job or digs for me, I again ended up in a convent, this time run by the Sisters of the Good Shepherd.

I was told it was a place where offenders went while waiting to go to court, but was reassured that it would only be for a few days until I found a live-in job. I hated every minute of my stay there. It was like a prison, and I shared a dormitory with about twenty other girls.

We had to be on our knees, on the floor, at six o'clock every morning to say prayers. We were then led to the chapel for Mass, had breakfast and then spent all day in the laundry-room, where my job was to press shirts. No visitors, no mail, no outside communication whatsoever.

I befriended an old lady there, who had been institutionalised many years before. She was a mute and she was blind. She taught me how to read her hand, and I would sit and tell her stories, while she would speak of the dark world she was living in. I felt very stupid about complaining of my existence.

The weeks multiplied into months. Girls faces changed every week, as they left to be dealt with by the courts.

It was very difficult to get to see the Mother Superior; I tried so often to find out why I hadn't even had a visit from my Welfare Officer. So, after a year of captivity, I decided to run away.

It was a really bad winter's night, but I managed to climb out of a small window onto the roof of the dormitory. It was snowing and icy cold. I was wearing only a cotton shift dress, shoes and socks; the shoes had been given to me for my work in the laundry-room and they were red and shiny. I loved those shoes.

I clambered down the drain-pipe and headed for the main road, which was a long way up the drive. I didn't know how far, it had been such a long time since my arrival.

I didn't even get as far as the main gate. Two of the auxiliary sisters were walking down the drive and saw me. I must have looked a pretty sight. There wasn't much of me; I'd lost the weight I'd put on in Dunoon and I was only four feet ten, so any great leap for freedom would have been impossible. I had no idea where I was heading, all I knew was that the convent was in Greenock.

I was taken to the Mother Superior's study and couldn't stop chittering with the cold and nerves; I didn't know which was the worst. She shrank me with one look. "What do you think you're playing at?" Not a sound came from me; I was petrified. "So you are the one who sees people? Well let them keep you company tonight." With a swish of her habit, she was gone.

I was taken to the punishment room. A dark, dank, unlit toilet which was outside in the convent grounds. One of the auxiliary nuns held a torchlight until I was safely locked in, and away they went, leaving me there in the cold and the dark for the rest of the night. There was not even a chair, so I had to sit on the cold, damp floor. This made me ill, but I still had my duties to carry out; after all, I caused it with my own stupidity!

Not long after this incident, I was called to the Mother Superior's office again, where she told me that she had made enquiries of the Glasgow Welfare Department, and informed me that my Welfare Officer had died and, as there were so many children to sort out, they hadn't got round to me yet. However, it should not take long now that they were aware that I was there. I'd been forgotten, so I was to remain there until they came for me.

I left the convent early in 1959, when I was seventeen years old, and was taken to a family-run hotel in Greenock, overlooking the sea, where I was to be the general help. The family were very nice to me, and I soon settled. I was so happy to be away from that Convent.

I was paid ten shillings plus my keep. I had become very introverted, so was content to spend my leisure time drawing, and riding a bicycle which was at my disposal. The view from the hotel was lovely, and I spent a lot of time looking out to sea, day-dreaming. Some day, I'll find my own mother and everything'll be all right. Dreams are wonderful things; where would we be without them?

As the hotel was outside of Greenock, I never ventured as far as the town and didn't have any friends. There was no one of my age.

Summer was busy, and I enjoyed my work. I would do the lounge first thing in the morning, then start the bedrooms and help in the kitchen. My health was good; I was very fortunate. Perhaps my nerves were not as good as they might have been but, other than that, I was fine.

I began saving to take a trip home to Dunoon, which was only a ferry ride away, and I wanted to go back looking prosperous and taking presents for everybody. I would take my trip when the season eased off and I could be spared.

"Margaret, you've got visitors," Betty called.

I was in the kitchen helping with the washing up after lunch.

Visitors! Who on earth could possibly be visiting

me? Quickly, I headed towards reception.

I froze in my tracks. There were Esther Hutchison, Auntie Peg, and Auntie Anne from London. My first reaction was to run; I didn't need this. Auntie Anne approached me. I did love her, she was kindness itself, and I'm sure she had never known what had been going on.

"Let's go to your room and have a chat."

It's Dad, I thought, what's happened to Dad? He was the only one I really cared about.

I led her to my room.

"Darling, your dad's OK, but he's had to have a lung removed. Your mum's beside herself with worry. Pat's away now, on the Empress of Canada, and Frank's not quite finished his apprenticeship. Mum does miss you, you know, and she needs you badly now; will you please come home?"

"I don't want to, Auntie Anne. I've had enough — you don't know what she's like!"

"I'm sure that, if we sit down and discuss this like adults, it will be all right."

I know, now, that Auntie Anne was the bait, the only person Mum knew I would listen to. That's why she brought her.

"What about the Welfare Department?" I said.

"They have said it's OK with them if you want to come back."

Of course, they didn't really care as long as I was somewhere until I was eighteen; after all, I was a liability! I gave in and went back. I couldn't settle, I didn't want to stay. There were too many memories for me at home.

My sanctuary had always been Rachel's house.

How things would have been different if I had been in that family. Rachel's mum was terrific, and they were all so close.

Mum still wouldn't consider my going into factory work, so Rachel and I started contacting hotels in Edinburgh. We finally got an interview at a hotel near the Waverley station. Rachel had been cheesed off in her job, and she felt like a change. Her mum was all for it, mine wasn't.

"If I get the job I could send you money home every week," I told her, "The wages are much better in Edinburgh." She wouldn't consider it.

Rachel's mum advised me to go for the interview anyway and, should we get the job, she was sure that Mum would come round. So, off we went without Mum's permission.

Chambermaids in the Coburn Hotel in Edinburgh! It was grand. We would live-in, and the pay was two pounds ten shillings.

"I'm going," I screamed. "You've persecuted me long enough and, if you do inform the Welfare, they'll never find me 'coz I'll keep on running."

"You ungrateful bitch," she screamed at me. "After all I've done for you! I took you in and gave you a home and this is how you repay me. You'll end up on the streets, lady, that's what'll happen to you!"

I ran off to stay at Rachel's until we left for Edinburgh.

Mum would not let me have any of my clothes, so Rachel's mum went to see her and returned to report that Mum had thrown everything belonging to me out in the dustbin. I couldn't care less; possessions didn't mean anything. I was determined never to go back.

So, Rachel and I shared clothes until I had saved enough to buy some.

Dad managed to get a message to me, letting me know when it would be safe for me to visit him in hospital. Mum was never told of my visits, and he reassured me that what I'd done was the best thing and that I wasn't to worry.

I was sad when he went back to Fife, as I didn't know when I would see him again. That was when I realised that he was frightened of Mum.

On our days off, Rachel and I would catch the train home to her mother's. On one of these trips, we boarded the bus from the station in Cowdenbeath and went upstairs. Mum was sitting up at the front.

God! Had she seen me? We crept back down the stairs, but she had spotted us and she came down, hurling abuse at me in front of everybody. She threw her shopping at me and, cornering me, she gave me a good hiding. No one interfered; she terrified everybody on that bus. That ended my visits to Fife. I couldn't take any more chances.

Ronnie started at the hotel as a porter and we fell in love straight away. He was the handsomest person I'd ever seen, and we married on the 1st of October, 1960. Our son, John, was born in February 1961. I was nineteen, Ronnie was sixteen.

Mum had come over to the hospital on the day my baby was born and she idolized him, did everything for him and suggested that she should take him across to Fife with her, to enable me to go back to work to help finances.

Throughout my pregnancy I hadn't even been to see a doctor. I was a healthy soul, so I went straight back to work, and Mum took John back to Fife when he was six weeks old. Did she think that James had come back? I don't know, all I do know is that she kept calling him by that name.

My marriage to Ronnie started going downhill, fast, so in 1965 I moved to Kent, vowing never to return to Scotland. I had taken all the humiliation, the violence and suffering I was going to take. This was the end of it, as far as I was concerned.

One of my school friends from St Columbus High had moved down to Deal and, in her letters, had invited me there should I ever feel the need. A few years before, I had helped her through an emotional situation, and she felt that, without my spirit guidance, she would never have pulled herself together.

As I sat on the coach from Edinburgh to Victoria, I was a very frightened soul. I'd never travelled anywhere on my own before and didn't know where I was going. I didn't even know if Margaret had received my letter, as I'd only sent it the day before, asking her to meet me in Deal at the coach's scheduled time of arrival. I'd left with one small suitcase containing just bare essentials. As the coach sped through the darkness, rain lashing at the windows, I was certain of only one thing: that I would never go back.

Feeling emotionally drained, and very sorry for myself, I began to question. Why had life been so cruel to me? I had never been wicked to anyone. What had I done to deserve such an existence? As I sat there, watching the smoke rising into the nightlights, the passengers smoking and reading their books and papers, a voice spoke to me, by now a familiar voice. My spirit friend. He'd never deserted me.

"You must pull yourself together. There are many, many, people far worse off than you."

"Don't give me that," I interrupted. "I'm fed up with you always telling me I'll be all right. Everything I do is wrong, and I'm not going to listen to you any more. I wish I'd drowned myself years ago."

"Margaret, as time goes by, you will come to understand: the gift is not for you."

Suddenly, I felt a warmth around me. A spirit cuddle. The gift is not for me? I didn't understand. However, I began to relax. Of course, you will realise that my discussions with the spirit side are always by thought. There is no need to use speech as we know it. The five senses are not used in spirit communication. The sixth sense is required.

He did not say any more, my nameless, faceless friend. I woke with a start, the sun streaming in through the windows. I sat up and looked out. We were speeding along a street, passengers were moving around, collecting their belongings from the luggage rack, while a queue formed at the toilet. I looked ahead at the clock; it was 7.20 a.m. We were almost at Victoria Station.

Heading into the bustle of the coach station, I began to tremble. People were laughing and chatting, everyone heading for their own destination, for whatever reasons. I wasn't even certain of my destination. I soon found the stand for Deal and felt some relief on entering the coach. If this is London, I thought, they can keep it! It frightened me so. I'd never seen so many people; they were like ants, all hustling and bustling around.

City life would not suit me at all! The poor pigeons looking for food; I'd never seen so many, and spotted a few with only one leg, scurrying around, the coaches missing them by inches. I felt sad for these poor creatures.

It wasn't long before the coach was speeding through the Kent countryside. The scenery was lovely, but my thoughts were not on enjoying the view. I was praying that Margaret would be at my destination. I dreaded the thought that she might not be there, might not even have received my letter.

We eventually pulled into the station and I peered at all the faces waiting. I couldn't see her anywhere! Nervously, I left the coach. No, she wasn't there. I fumbled in my bag to find her address. Oh dear! What do I do? Should I wait a while? Yes, that's what I'll do. What if she doesn't live here any more? What if she has moved away? Where will I go? I don't know anybody and I've got one pound and ten shillings between me and poverty.

I was dying for a cup of tea. My throat was parched, I'd got no cigarettes, and couldn't afford to buy any. I sat down helplessly and tried to think straight, looking around all the time. I must have looked a pitiful sight; I was as thin as a rake, only six and a half stone.

The station grew quieter as people and transport moved on. Suddenly I heard her, "Yoohoo, Margaret!" I jumped up from my little suitcase and there she was, running towards me. We hugged each other and both burst into tears.

"I thought you hadn't got my letter," I cried, relief sweeping over me.

Margaret replied, "I've only just got it; I go to my wee job in the mornings before the post arrives, and I've run all the way up here. I've been so worried. Well, come on," she said, "let's get you home. Then we'll have a nice cup of tea."

With that, off we went. I felt the tiredness leave me and a surge of hope replace it. Margaret's flat was one large room above a shop. Access to it was through the shop. She had moved to Deal with her son, Gordon, to stay with her newly-married mother. Sadly, things had not worked out, so she'd moved into this room, but she was both cheery and contented.

Although I'd known Margaret since childhood, it was her mum, Jean, and my mum, who had become friends. Everywhere her mum went, Margaret went. I liked Jean very much; to me, she was modern and young at heart. I liked going to their house. Margaret told her mum everything; they were a good team.

I remember that, when my periods started, I had been terrified to tell my mum in case I got into trouble, so it was Jean I told, who in turn told my mum. I was so embarrassed. I was casually thrown a sanitary belt and towels, while my brothers were in the room, with Mum saying, "You will now be using these till you are about fifty and, if you let a man near you now, you'll find yourself pregnant, so don't come to me complaining. The curse is on you now, and you have been warned." I was twelve years old.

I had never been allowed to watch anything on TV concerning birth or sex. Of course, Margaret, who was a year older than I, knew everything; her mother had let her watch it all. I did admire her knowledge of things, being, myself, so ignorant of the facts of life. This subject had been taboo in our home and this was, perhaps, one of the reasons I had liked going to her house.

Margaret's dad was a lovely person, too, a miner just like mine. There were also two brothers, and laughter seemed to reign there. I especially liked her elder brother Pat, who was in the Black Watch and looked so smart in his uniform and was always full of life.

Pat used to enjoy brushing my hair, while we all sat listening to Slim Whitman and a variety of Country and Western singers. We loved the music; without music, where would we be?

I had been sitting one day sadly watching him packing-up ready to go back to the Black Watch. I did love his fussing and the stories he told, all tales of course.

With a twinkle in his eye, he had said to me, "Next time I'm on leave I'm going to elope with you. We're going to Hawaii - you'll fit in well with your long black hair. We'll swap our clothes for grass skirts and garlands, and we'll laze in the sun all day."

Right, I had thought excitedly, my future is assured! Jean had burst out laughing.

"Don't take any notice of him, hen, his head is always in the clouds without putting yours there as well."

Next time he came home on leave he had taken Margaret and me to the pictures to see Oklahoma. That was the nearest I got to my Hawaiian wedding. A few weeks later he got married.

"Where's John?" Margaret asked.

"I couldn't bring him out of Scotland, I was too scared. It felt like I would be stealing him. I put a letter in the post to Mum when I sent yours, asking her to pick him up and look after him until I could sort something out."

My brother, Frank, had been staying with us in Edinburgh, as he'd finished his training but had been having a lot of trouble with his ears. There was a doctor coming from London to perform an operation on him but he didn't want Mum to know too much, so he had told her that work opportunities were greater in Edinburgh. He'd had enough of the pit. Unfortunately, the operation was unsuccessful. My heart went out to him, he was a good lad.

I'd received a letter from Mum during that time, in which she'd told me she'd had a dream that Frank was in hospital and she was worried. Would I let her know if everything was all right? I had written back to say that it was just a silly dream, and that Frank was fine and had secured a good job as foreman in an engineering works in Leith, which was true. She had been given the facts in her dream. Later, I told her the whole truth.

Before I left for Kent, I'd left John a few doors away playing with his pal. I'd told his pal's mum that I had to go to Princes Street, but that Frank and Ronnie would be home in about an hour.

I'd confided in only one person, and that was my boss. I'd been working part-time in a Casino club and had been able to take John with me. My boss was very supportive, saying how sorry he was that I was going and that, if he could help in any way, I was to get in touch. My job would remain open should I want to come back.

"John will be fine at Mum's," I told Margaret. "She's never going to forgive me for walking out, anyway, but I couldn't take John out of her life. I just hope that one day she'll understand."

Margaret knew Mum only too well, and looked at me sympathetically.

"She won't ever give him back, you know."

"Yes," I murmured, "but I'll have to cross that bridge when I come to it."

I slept like a baby that first night in Kent, and woke up next morning feeling as if a weight had been lifted from me. Right! First I must get a job, and save as much as possible to provide a home for myself and my son. So, off I went to try the hotels that Margaret had told me about; after all, I was a good chambermaid. The first hotel accepted me, and I started work two days after my arrival in Deal.

Mrs Johnson arrived at the hotel the following week. She was a sad looking, but pleasant, soul. She'd be staying a few days only.

"Whatever are you doing chamber-maiding?" she remarked. "With your looks, you should be in films. Hasn't anyone told you that you look like Elizabeth Taylor?"

"Yes, everybody tells me that." I smiled, remembering that people used to think that she might be a relation of mine, as I did look very much like her. I never took this as a compliment, just as confirmation that the resemblance was there.

"I'd love a cup of tea," said Mrs Johnson.

"I'll go and get you one." And off I went to fetch it. Re-entering the room, I found her with company.

Putting the tray down, I asked her if she would like me to bring another cup.

"What for, dear?"

"For the gentleman."

She stared at me. "What gentleman?"

I looked towards the man sitting on the chair and realised the truth.

"Oh, I am sorry, I was mistaken." I headed quickly for the door.

"Just a minute dear."

Gosh, I thought, how do I get out of this?

"Sit down," she said, kindly but firmly, and I obeyed. "Tell me who you saw."

"Who are you?" I asked, mentally.

"I'm her husband, please tell her I'm all right over here."

I repeated what he'd said and she burst into tears. I jumped up and put my arms around her. "There, there, it's all right. He's fine and just wants you to know."

It turned out that he'd passed three weeks previously, after a long illness.

"I'd better be about my duties, Mrs Johnson, but I'll pop in and see you before I leave." And I did. I asked her to kindly not mention what had happened, to anyone else at the hotel, in case I got into trouble.

Walking back along the sea front, I was very worried. What if she mentions it and I lose my job? Next time something like this happens, I'll keep quiet. But it's not that easy, as it's very difficult to tell the difference between spirit people and we who are solid. My mind was full of troubled thoughts as I continued to walk along the dark, deserted promenade.

It was the middle of October and the sea was rushing noisily up the shingled beach. What was that? I could hear footsteps. Looking round, I saw no one in the half-darkness of the street-lights, so I hastened my steps. My heart started pounding as I cut down one of the small side-streets. The footsteps seemed to be getting closer; as mine quickened, so did they. I began to run.

Suddenly, I was grabbed from behind. Only absolute fear prevented me from screaming. I was forced around and came face-to-face with my husband, Ronnie. He'd found me. My mother had told him where I was. Ronnie had brought John with him, and John was already at Margaret's.

The end result was that I felt I could not go back to Scotland, so John and I remained in Deal. I have no wish to cause any distress to Ronnie's parents, whom I love dearly, but the fact remains that we were both too young for the responsibility of marriage.

I next saw Ronnie ten years later just prior to his death in 1977, at the age of thirty-two. He would never accept that there was anything after death, and used to say, "When you're dead, you're dead, kaput!" He was to prove, from the spirit side, just how wrong his sceptical remarks had been!

Now I was in a quandary. I couldn't keep my job, as the hours arranged for me were from 7 am until 3 pm, and then from 5 to 7 pm, so I found myself sitting in the DHSS office asking for help for my son and myself. Margaret's landlord would not entertain allowing four of us to live in one room. There are many, many people who know how difficult it is for anyone with a child to find accommodation, let alone a job. So there I was, on the streets, with nowhere at all to go.

Besides, the DHSS told me, I had put myself in this position. I still had a good home in Edinburgh, so perhaps I should return and sort something out there. No way. I had made a break. A return journey, I would never make.

I could not afford to go into bed and breakfast so, that first night, John and I settled down under cover on Deal pier. It was a cold, cold night. I'll never forget it. As John slept peacefully cuddled up to me, I sat awake all night, too scared to sleep, telling myself we'd find something in the morning.

It would have put Margaret's tenancy in jeopardy, had I remained in her room above the shop to be found by the landlord. John dashed along the shingled beach, proudly presenting me with the dead fish he'd found. That raw fish was to be our lunch. Even today, memories flood back whenever I eat fish, a dish I've only been able to face again during the last six years or so.

I met Margaret as we'd arranged, and she told me of a lady who might be able to help. Off we went. My hopes were raised a little as we arrived at her house. "It could only be for a little while," she said, "until the season begins," and gave us a room. The rent was one pound ten shillings. At least for now, we'd got a roof over our heads.

Margaret took John for a few hours to allow me to get some sleep. I wearily sat on the bed, feeling too tired to care about anything any more. But it was no good feeling sorry for myself, this was my choice. I looked in the cracked mirror on the wall and felt like an old woman. In one week, my black hair had turned to grey.

I managed to get John into the local primary school. He was a happy little soul.

Christmas was not too far away, and I was very worried. I couldn't afford anything. I'd only got about ten shillings left from the hotel job I'd had to give up. Back I went to the DHSS. I explained my change of circumstances, which they were not really interested in. The office was a dreadful place, bare and cold, but they were only doing their jobs, I suppose.

I'd always worked since I was fifteen and had never had any dealing with either unemployment or social security departments. I felt like a beggar. As most people know, you are not dealt with in five minutes at the DHSS, and I was asked to wait to see some gentleman.

After sitting for ages and ages, I was called in to see this man. As I sat listening to him, I saw a lady appear beside him; there was no way I was mentioning this apparition, so I ignored her. Her hair was black, her eyes were blue and she was very sad looking. She looked a bit like me, except that my hair was now embarrassingly grey. Although I was ignoring her, I could tell that her accent was German. The DHSS man was very sympathetic and said he would do what he could. I thanked him, and left.

That evening, I was telling Margaret of my visit and that I didn't know when or if I could get any money from them, when a knock came on the door. Expecting to see the landlady, I was quite taken aback to see this gentleman from the DHSS. He apologized for calling late, and asked if he could come in.

Margaret and I looked at each other, rather puzzled. The DHSS man admitted to me that this was not usually quite the way in which his department worked, but he had felt that I was an awfully worried woman and had therefore decided to deal with my case straight away. He produced a cheque for me to change first thing in the morning. I was completely overwhelmed, and thanked him very much.

Not satisfied with that, he then took his wallet out and handed me a five-pound note.

"To get some fish and chips tonight."

Tears welled up in my eyes. This was the first kindness I'd ever been shown by a stranger.

Then he said, "When you were sitting across the table from me, this morning, you reminded me so much of someone who was very dear to me once, but she was from Germany, not Scotland."

There was a hint of a tear in his eye as he bade us goodnight. I was flabbergasted, but now I understood.

"He really fancies you," Margaret sniggered.

"Oh, I don't think so," I replied, thanking that wonderful lady on the spirit side.

"Come on, let's get down to the chip shop." I had chicken and chips, Margaret had cod.

Tomorrow, I thought, I'm going to buy some hair colour and get rid of this grey. I've been using it ever since.

I often wonder if that gentleman ever realised what urged him to do what he did. I hope so. God bless him!

FIVE

Next morning, I was awfully sick. I had a fever and my whole body was aching. I had never felt so bad, physically; I was never ill. Somehow, I walked John to school and called in to see Margaret.

She looked after a house for a gentleman who was a producer at the BBC, and he only used his house at the weekend as he was in London all week. She took one look at me and told me to go and see a doctor.

"I don't need a doctor. I'll be OK, it's just the 'flu or something."

Of course, my chicken and chips from the night before had been the most I'd eaten for four or five days. Although I had made sure John was eating, I'd gone without myself, and this had made me ill. The fact that I was able to buy some food and pay the rent made me think positively about my situation, so a few days and aspirins later I was feeling far better.

I had asked John what he would like from Father Christmas; he wanted a budgie. Christmas Eve was depressing. It would have been all right if I hadn't been able to hear the laughter coming from downstairs, where the landlady's entire family had gathered for the celebrations. John was fast asleep; no doubt, like any other child, dreaming about what he was going to get from Santa.

We had no radio or TV, and Margaret and Gordon had gone to her mother's for Christmas. I knew her mother would have liked to have invited us, but there was her new husband to consider and things had not been going too well for her. However, Christmas morning dawned and John excitedly took the cover from the bird-cage, which I had managed to find in a second-hand shop.

So, on Christmas Day 1966, Charlie joined our family. That little budgie was a godsend. We chatted away to him, day in and day out. It wasn't long before he was talking ten to the dozen!

"What are you Charlie? What are you?"

"Charlie's a silly little boy," he would chirp back.

His cage was never closed; he'd wander all over, wherever the fancy took him.

With New Year a few days away, Margaret came round; Gordon was staying on at her Mum's. "Perhaps we could go for a drink if you can get a baby-sitter."

Go out, I thought, that would be nice. Other than the odd occasion out with Ronnie to play Bingo, I'd been out, socially, only once in five years. I didn't drink, so going to the pub didn't hold any interest for me.

The following morning, talking to my landlady, I asked her if she knew anyone who would baby-sit for me. She suggested that, if I put John to bed before I went out, she would listen for him. I excitedly dressed for my evening out, and felt a mixture of nerves and excitement as we entered the pub. Margaret said we would make it a double celebration – New Year, and my birthday on the 6th of January the following week, when I would be twenty-four. And this was my first visit to a pub with another girl! Mum and Dad had enjoyed a drink and a good old singsong, and used to spend many hours at the Miners Institute in Fife with family and friends.

I didn't mind singing, it was just that I did not like the taste of drink.

"What are you having?" Margaret asked.

"Gosh, I don't know, what do you think?"

"Well, I drink gin and orange."

"Then I'll try the same as you."

Everybody in the pub was enjoying themselves.

"You stand there and I'll go and get the drinks."

"No, I'll come with you," I said. I didn't want to be left standing by myself. We moved to a couple of vacant seats and sipped our drinks; I didn't like mine, but I drank it anyway and began to enjoy myself with the music and a group of lads who'd taken us into their company. They were a cheery bunch, all from the Deal Barracks.

We didn't stay 'til closing time because I didn't want to be too late and, besides, the drink was going for me in a merry sort of way. We bade the lads goodnight, promising we would see them the following week.

Next morning, my head was throbbing. My first morning-after-the-night-before had arrived, and I'd only had three drinks! However, I decided that it would be my last.

The weeks went by, my life revolving about John. We were happy and content. The four of us went everywhere together: Margaret, John, Gordon and I.

It was now March, and the weather was pleasant. Margaret had heard from her ex-husband, who wanted Gordon to go and stay for a while in his home town of Liverpool. Gordon was excited at the prospect of seeing his father again; Alan had been in the Navy and had met Margaret when the Ark Royal had been in Rosyth.

After marrying, Margaret had lived in Malta for a few years as a Navy wife and Gordon had been born there. Things hadn't worked out. Margaret had soon found out that Alan had another 'wife' in Liverpool, so Margaret and Gordon had gone to stay with me in Edinburgh.

A few days later, Gordon left to stay with his dad. John had been invited to stay one Saturday night with a school chum, so it was an opportunity for Margaret and I to go out, and we did.

That night, I met Bob (not real name), who was handsome and smart. We hit it off straight away; he was fun to be with, and we shared the same sense of humour. Bob was in the CID, and took me to places I never would have gone to myself. Even though I sensed all was not right, I ignored this; I was well and truly smitten.

I didn't know how much my marriage breakup had affected me psychologically. However, this soon came to light when Bob went to kiss me; I just froze. I had sworn never to get close to any man again. I certainly had a problem, but he was very understanding and didn't push me, for which I was grateful. We would spend most evenings together, when he would bring me bits and pieces belonging to other people and I would read them. He reckoned that it was a remarkable gift that I had, and was amazed that I could go into so much detail about peoples' lives without ever even meeting them. As much as he tried, however, he couldn't do it himself.

I told him everything about my life. I did love this guy, more than life itself, and didn't question his love for me. I had not thought too much about the season almost at hand and my landlady's warning that I could only stay until it started, and now she needed my room for visitors. I needed to find other digs for myself and John; I told myself that everything would be all right. Bob would sort something out.

Margaret was not so sure; she hadn't taken to Bob at all. She was much more worldly-wise than me and, in her own way, she was trying to protect me.

"Why doesn't he ever take you to his place?" she asked.

"Well, I don't know. Is it important?" I replied.

"It could be; how can you be certain he's not married?"

"Because he told me his wife divorced him when she caught him with someone else. It was all his fault, he's learnt his lesson, and said he would never let it happen again. Besides, you know I won't ever sleep with him, so he can't be just after that one thing."

"Well," Margaret replied. "I think he is. You're a challenge to him - you're probably the first woman he's had difficulty getting into bed, and he'll stay around until he does."

"God, you're a sick person, Margaret, you don't know what you're saying."

"Well," she said, "time will tell."

"You can't be right. Doesn't he take me to dinner with other guys on the force?" I argued.

"Oh yes, he does, but coppers stick together."

"Oh, you are unbelievable!" In all the years we had known each other, this was our very first argument.

I watched Bob's face anxiously when I told him we'd got to move. "Can you help?" I asked.

"Well there'd be no problem finding you some place alone, but for both you and John, it would be difficult. You know what it was like finding this room; why don't you send him back to his father and let him do some of the worrying for a change? After all, it's his fault you're in this predicament."

"Get out of here," I screamed. "I never want to see you again!"

He didn't answer, but left, closing the door quietly behind him. I was angry and hurt and about to be homeless again. I couldn't handle it. I spent all of the next day looking for a room, to no avail.

"Perhaps the Social Services can help," my landlady suggested.

"It's worth a try."

So off I went to them.

The only thing they could suggest was for John and me to go into a halfway house for the time being.

"What's that?" I asked. God, I was dumb.

"A place for battered wives and their children, but at least it's somewhere to stay."

"How long do you expect me to stay there?" I cried.

"Until the season ends, and back again when it starts."

The woman just looked at me. "Well, it's the best I can offer," she said, "other than your son going into care."

"Well that's not good enough," I snapped, and stormed out of her office. John go into care? I'd kill myself before I'd let that happen.

All of my life I'd been ordered about, everybody

telling me what to do. I had been both physically and mentally abused. I just couldn't take this, it was too much for me. So, without any more thought on the subject, I arranged a one-way ticket for John to go back to Edinburgh. One thing Bob had been right about: let Ronnie do the worrying for a change.

I told John he was going on a holiday to his Gran's, in just the same way Gordon had gone to his dad's, and he was thrilled to bits. He was jumping with excitement as we travelled up to Victoria. I had a word with the coach driver, then scanned the faces of the people travelling. I found a couple who I felt might look after him for me and they kindly agreed, giving me their address and telephone number. I had given the driver my mother-in-law's address and money for a taxi for John to be taken there. It was very difficult to try and hide from him how upset I was.

As the coach left Victoria for Edinburgh, I could see his small, beaming face pressed up against the window. I blew him a kiss, then just broke down and cried and cried.

A woman stopped and asked me what was the matter, and I blurted out my story.

"Let's go and have a cuppa, my love," she said, "and we'll talk about it."

She was very kind and understanding, and we talked for about two hours. I don't think it made me feel any better, but I got it out of my system.

"You have done what you think is best for the boy, love, and I think I would have done the same. You just need some breathing-space."

"But I did this in anger," I wept.

"Well, perhaps anger and frustration were the motives you needed; now try to stop worrying. He's going back to family, and he'll be fine. Believe me, children are adaptable! You haven't lost him, you're just not in a position to take care of him properly, but you'll have him back one day, I know you will. Take my address and let me know how you are doing from time to time."

The communication between Freda and myself lasted for eight years until her death in 1974.

On my way back to Deal, the words of my spirit friend kept coming into my head. 'The gift is not for me. The gift is not for me.'

As there were just two of us, now, Margaret's landlord let me move in. I couldn't wait for the following evening to phone a neighbour of Jean's. John had arrived safely; the couple who had looked after him on the coach had taken him to her house in the taxi. They also lived in Edinburgh. I was assured that he was fine, and I was not to worry. I was so relieved.

Then I phoned the couple and thanked them very much; they said that John had been as good as gold.

Arm-in-arm, Margaret and I walked back to her room.

"Charlie, John is OK, so for now we are three."

I wasn't going to worry any more. John was safe and wouldn't be pushed from pillar to post. Margaret and I promised that we would always look after each other, whatever happened in life.

I got another hotel job and Margaret joined me.

On our way home each day, we noticed a car parked near the shop. We thought it rather strange. The two men sitting there always watched us. After about three days of this, we ran up to our room and peered out of the window, and saw the car moving away. This happened again during the following few days; each time, the car drove off soon after we had entered the shop. The mystery was soon solved. Bob had got a few of his CID pals to find out where I was.

We decided to approach the car when next we saw it, and Margaret asked the CID men why they were watching us. One replied, "Bob wants to know how his bird is doing."

"Tell him his bird is doing fine, thank you very much," I retorted.

The following day found Bob sitting outside my workplace.

"Let's talk," he said. I got in his car and we drove off. He told me he didn't want to lose me and, I suppose, all the other things I wanted to hear. I was his Liz Taylor who only starred in his life, and he'd got so many plans for our future, but first he wanted me to view a flat he'd found in Sandwich. It was a property belonging to a friend of his.

"Where I go, Margaret goes," I told him.

"Well, that's all right. There are two bedrooms so you can have one each. We'll go and look at it tomorrow."

The three of us arrived in Sandwich. It was a lovely flat and reasonable, too. Margaret and Gordon would have the larger bedroom, and there was also a separate kitchen and bathroom and a nice big garden. As it was too far from our present work, we decided we'd look for something closer. Bob's friends who owned the place lived downstairs, and the wife told Margaret she would see Gordon to school and back again, with her own child who was the same age. Bob paid a month's rent for us and so it was settled.

Margaret got in touch with Alan who told her that Gordon liked Liverpool so much that he wanted to stay permanently. After chatting to Gordon, it was decided he'd remain with his dad. Fate had dealt us another hand, another blow! We comforted each other. So much had happened in so short a time, and we had now both lost our children.

What did life hold in store? We were very uncertain. It was then that I gave myself to Bob for the first time; I needed this man so much.

We secured a job at a Sandwich factory. I felt guilty at taking this job, remembering how Mum had said so many years ago she'd break my legs before letting me go into a factory. It was a small firm, where our job was to put wires into outboard motors, and we enjoyed it.

We were a happy group. At lunchtime, everyone rushed to the pub next door, where we would have a sandwich, the boys would have a pint and we'd all play darts.

Bob showed up most lunchtimes. He wanted me to consult a solicitor about a divorce, telling me it would take some time as I was now in England and it would have to be dealt with in Scotland. I wasn't ready for this, yet, so I kept putting it off. Besides, Margaret didn't think it was a good idea, and felt that my life was evolving around Bob too much. Where she was accepting invitations to go out socially with the boys and girls from work, I was not.

I had never led a single life and didn't feel the need to start one now. After all, I had all I wanted. I felt protected, something I'd never felt before.

During one of Margaret's weekend visits to Deal, she popped into the old address to see if there was any mail. We hadn't let anyone know of our change of address in case Ronnie found out, for obvious reasons. There was one letter for me. I hastily opened it, hoping it was news of John, but it was from one of my sisters-in-law, and did she tear me to pieces!

It was a terrible letter. I was a so-called mother who abandoned her son so that I could enjoy myself. It reduced me to tears. Margaret tore it up straight away, wrote on it, 'THIS HAS BEEN TREATED WITH THE CONTEMPT IT DESERVES,' and we posted it back. Bob persuaded me to put it out of my mind.

"Look here, at this," he said one evening, looking through the local paper.

The cinema in Deal would soon be showing a James Bond film and they were looking for two girls to advertise the forthcoming attraction.

"Why don't you apply?"

"What for?" I asked.

"Well, you'd get your picture in the paper. You'd also be taken out to dinner and earn a few bob."

"I don't think so."

"Go on, you could do with the break, it's something out of the ordinary."

"OK, I'll do it for a laugh, but I don't think for one minute that I'll be chosen."

"You're the best looking girl in Deal," he said.

He drove me down to the cinema, where auditions were being held. I found about thirty girls there. The end result was that another girl and myself were chosen to parade through Deal in our bikinis, advertising

James Bond. I felt so stupid, but it pleased Bob no end, especially when my picture was in the paper.

Not long after that, in fact early the following Sunday afternoon, the doorbell rang. On answering it, I found two women standing there. They asked for me.

"Yes, what do you want?"

The younger asked if she might come in, as she wanted to talk to me.

"Please do," I replied, inviting them in. I offered them a cup of tea, but they declined.

"I shall come to the point," the younger remarked, "I believe you are the girl my husband has been seeing," she said.

"I'm sorry, you must be mistaken." She was a very attractive woman, a few years older than myself.

Then she asked, "Are you going out with Bob so-and-so?"

"Yes I am, but he's not married."

"He is too! He is married to me."

You could have knocked me down with a feather. He had lied to me all along. The other lady was her mother. They told me that he had been found out so many times before, and proceeded to give me all the details.

His wife then showed me a letter, which was supposedly from me, asking her to give him up. She told me she knew it was written by him; he'd just changed his writing.

I couldn't believe he could be capable of doing such a thing, but he obviously was. He hadn't known they were coming to see me. I couldn't apologize enough, and promised I'd give him up straight away.

When he arrived that evening, he was eagerly going

on about us emigrating to Australia.

"Bob, don't you think your wife will have something to say about that?"

He looked at me and asked what I was talking about; I told him, and he denied it was his wife, but a woman who'd been after him for ages.

I'd had my first taste of the shadier side of life and I did not like it one bit. I told him to leave, and that I wouldn't be seeing him any more.

He pestered me at the flat and at work, so Margaret and I decided to move on.

SIX

We found a flat in Ramsgate and another hotel job. Bob was out of my life; I'd learnt my lesson the hard way. I haven't set eyes on him to this day, but often wonder if his wife stayed with him. We loved our job, beginning as chamber maids and ending up as joint housekeepers.

Every day was fun. There were students of English staying in the hotel; they came from Persia, Germany and France and they all ended up coming to me with their problems.

It all began with one spurned in love by an English girl; I told him he would meet another girl a few days later and be happy with her, and he did. So the word got around, and yours truly ended up with a brigade of guys with problems.

A new girl started in the laundry and I felt very sorry for her. She did her work, but never said anything until one day, out of the blue, I said, "Jenny, why don't you leave him, you know things are never going to change unless you are strong." My 'voice' had spoken.

"How do you know what's wrong?" she said.

"I just know, my love."

So we talked, and a few weeks later Jenny left her miserable life. She became cheerful, did herself up and began to regain her confidence.

"If it hadn't been for you, Margaret, I would never

have found the courage to leave; it was something that I'd only ever dreamed about."

A few years later found her happily married, with the child her ex-husband had refused to let her have. Since then, she's had two more.

Our boss opened up a gaming casino upstairs and, on the opening night, we dolled ourselves up and went to have a look. The only gambling that I'd ever done was the odd sixpence bet with my mother-in-law on the horses and a few visits to Bingo. Margaret had never gambled.

On entering the Casino we were faced by two doormen, about six-foot-two and broad with it. "Good evening ladies," one said politely. We burst out giggling.

"We work here," I replied, "so we don't need your airs and graces."

We introduced ourselves to Mick and Peter, laughingly saying, "At ease, boys; on our wages you won't be getting much from us."

The buffet, which immediately caught our eyes, was fit for a king. The students all worked as chefs or waiters in the school, which was also the biggest hotel in Ramsgate, and, in return, they received their English lessons. They did look smart, all poshed up for the occasion.

We mingled with the invited guests. The women were dripping with gold and smelled to high heaven, all talking with plums in their mouths, and the men all chatted away about everything in general and nothing in particular.

We ventured to the bar. "Eh'll have a straight scotch, dear," said the lady perched on the bar stool, seven parts to the wind already.

"Thank you, Modom," replied Steve, looking at us and trying not to laugh at us silently imitating his 'Modom' behind her back.

"And what would you two ladies like to drink?" he asked, with a 'don't you dare try it' look on his face.

"Eh'll have a straight scotch too, please," in my best English voice, "and my friend will be eternally grateful for a G and T; she's had six already and is just getting the taste."

Margaret elbowed me in the side, as the lady, perched precariously on her stool, looked at her approvingly and smiled. It was the first time I had tried scotch and it took my breath away.

"Barman, put some orange in that for me."

Steve looked in wonder. "Orange, Modom?"

"Yes, my man, orange." It was unheard of, but it wasn't a bad taste. So that has been my drink ever since.

Our bar stool friend had captured Margaret for a blether, I guess happy to meet a guest with a similar capacity for liquor.

Margaret gave me a black look, as I excused myself to go and see how the gambling was doing.

While watching the roulette wheel spinning, a voice said, "Having a bet?" It was Mick from the door.

"No, I'm just watching."

With that, he handed me two and six.

"See if you can win with that."

I scanned the board and placed my bet. It won at eight to one. I moved the lot, up it came again.

I was getting excited now, as in no time at all I had thirty quid. My weekly wages were three pounds two and six, so I was loaded. Other punters began to follow me and were winning as well. Being a canny Scot, I didn't push my luck.

Next day Margaret and I had a good spend up on some new clothes. The Boss sent for me and told me I'd cost him a packet.

"Don't blame me," I said, "I was just lucky."

He laughed and said, "Let's see if you're lucky tonight."

"Oh I don't intend making a habit of this," I said, "I'm not that daft."

We were back that night, on went my two and sixpence, and up it came.

Rezer, the croupier, said, "You're in good company tonight. Do you know who that is over there?"

Peering across the table I spotted Lance Percival, and next to him sat Sir Billy Butlin. After my bets had come up about another six times, most of the punters followed me again and we lost. Every time after that we lost.

I got fed up and left the table, headed for Lance Percival, and asked for his autograph. He wrote it on my arm, then bought me a drink. "What number do you think?" he said.

"Number six." He put a lot of money on. Up it came, and I received a generous tip from the kind gentleman. Away I went to change the chips.

The Boss stopped me. "Don't you do that again, Margaret."

"Do what?"

"Tell anyone which number to play."

"Why not?"

"Just don't, or you and I will fall out."

"I've already lost interest in your tables anyway, so you can stuff them," and off I walked. Later, I was told that I had been used as a plant.

Some days later, while I was sitting and having a cuppa in the still room, a woman in her fifties walked in.

"I'm looking for Margaret."

"Which one?" I asked.

"The one that tells the future."

"I don't tell the future, hen, but what is it that you want?"

"I'm in trouble, and I need your advice."

"Well sit down, and I'll pour you a cuppa."

As she began to pour out her troubles, I found myself stopping her and telling her what was wrong.

"How do you know that?" she asked, amazed.

"I just know, that's all," and I went on to tell her what she should do. She left a lot happier than when she came in. A few days later, she phoned to say the situation had turned out just as I said it would; even I was surprised! From then on, various people would come looking for me, all finding the results they had been given.

One Saturday night, we decided to go over to Butlins in Margate. When we arrived, there was a band playing, a trio it was, and different people were getting up and singing a song. The atmosphere was great. All the wrestlers were arriving after their bouts at the Oval, across the road. Margaret suggested I get up and sing, so I did.

During the band's interval, the leader came over to me and said, "You can belt out a song, but you shouldn't try to copy Kitty Wells."

"Who's Kitty Wells, I've never heard of her," I replied.

"Well, for never hearing of her, you don't half sound like her! Anyway, would you like a job with the band?"

"I've got a job, thanks."

"I don't think you realize, but all the singers before you were auditioning to sing with us."

"Oh, I'm very sorry, I didn't realize."

"Well, you had the crowd asking for more, so what would you say, then, to being our non-resident singer on Saturday nights? I'll pay you five pounds for two songs."

"What time do you want me here?" I laughed.

So it was that I started with the Len Abedge Trio on Saturday nights. According to Len, Susan Maughan had started her career with them. They were a great bunch and we looked forward to our Saturdays at Butlins.

Tuesdays, our hotel held a dance with a band, and our housekeeper Mrs Kirby, a divorcee, Margaret and myself would take over for a laugh. I was on drums, Margaret was on piano and Mrs K on guitar. None of us could play properly, but we had terrific fun.

When any fellas chatted us up, we asked them to go and talk to our mum, Mrs Kirby. It was all good clean fun and we made lots of friends.

One of the hotel's ex-teachers had joined Britain Radio as a DJ, and was going under the name of Gordon Bennet, so we would listen intently to the radio for him to say hello to us and play our previously-arranged request.

I had always kept a diary as I had always intended

to write a book. Each time I started on the book, my 'voice' would tell me to wait until I had something to say. I felt that, by now, I had more than a book's worth to say, but he said, "You will write a book, one day. Keep your diaries till then. The time is not yet." So I kept my diaries.

When I received my mother's instructions from the spirit side, I rescued the dusty and faded diaries. I understand now why I was told to keep them.

Through this untroubled period in my life, my thoughts were sent out to my son every day. I would periodically parcel up a selection of toys and send them, but excluding my address and always having the parcel posted from Deal.

It was now almost Christmas 1966. Mick, the doorman from the Casino, had always turned up at Butlins on Saturday nights and we invited him into our company. He was a smashing bloke, always on his own. The hotel had quietened down, due to the time of the year. Mrs Kirby had moved in with a guy she'd got involved with, and Margaret and I were joint housekeepers.

One evening, Mick asked me out for a drink. He worked driving a machine during the day, and did a few evenings at the Casino.

"Well, Mick, you know: if I go, Margaret goes too."

This was standard practice; we would never go out with any fellahs unless we went together and came home together. The fellahs didn't mind, as it was always arranged as a foursome and we did have a good laugh. It also stopped any nonsense.

"You can trust me," Mick said. "I wouldn't harm you."

I already knew that, as did Margaret, so Mick and I went for a drink alone. During our conversation, Mick admitted he was surprised I wasn't married yet. I held up my left hand and said, "What do you think this is, Mick?"

"It's a wedding ring."

"That's right, I'm already married." I had always worn my ring. I didn't see any reason not to.

"So this means I can't marry you, then?" trying to hide his embarrassment.

"You, and a hundred like you," I laughed.

I liked him.

Christmas was rather busy at the hotel and staff were short; Margaret and I were working more or less around the clock. We had moved into the hotel from the flat, some time before, for convenience, and found it had not really been a good idea. We were too available.

Feeling rather depressed, my mind took me back to last Christmas and I shuddered at the thought. A lonely feeling crept over me as I wondered where I would find myself next Christmas.

By the 30th of December we were cheesed off with washing, ironing and doing our bedrooms. Our complaining to the Manageress ended up in a row and we left next day. We had nowhere to live, so I phoned Mick and asked if he knew of anywhere. He said we would be welcome to stay at his mother's.

So, December the 31st found us living in Margate. New Year came and went, and I managed to find work as a cashier at a well-known food store. Margaret started as an auxiliary nurse at the local hospital.

My mother had sent a birthday card and a letter to

Deal. The olive branch had been offered, and I felt then that any bitterness from the past should be thrown away now. So we began to communicate by post.

She hadn't seen John at all, and told me that Ronnie had given up our home and was living with someone else. So Frank had moved back home. While sailing on the Canberra, on which he was second engineer, Pat had met an English girl, on her way to spend a year nursing in Canada, and they had been married there. He had now left the Merchant Navy and was working for Ford in Toronto. Dad was doing well with the lung he had left.

I was pleased to have had some news after such a long time, and decided I could now start divorce proceedings. My only worry was, would I get custody of my son?

Although we had left Ramsgate, we had many friends there, so we continued to visit the hotel and were always invited to parties, weddings etc. They did miss us, saying the laughter had left with us, and we were always being asked to work there again. We declined.

Margaret loved her hospital work, so, on her insistence, I applied for a job there too. We shared a bedroom at Mick's mum's, but rather felt we were in the way. His mum, a widow, also worked at the hospital, but each time we suggested getting a flat, Mick intervened, saying we were fine there. So we stayed put.

Margaret met a nice chap and I was courting Mick. During this time, I felt the urge to find my father.

Assuming my surname was his, I wrote to the Glasgow Police Headquarters for help. They, in turn, passed my enquiry on to a sister of his, who informed me that he had been killed in a road accident in 1949. Neither she, nor any of her family, had had any knowledge of my existence.

Well, that was that. The end of my dreams. Reality had intervened. Some weeks later, however, she wrote again. While discussing me with other members of the family, she had established that her brother was not, in fact, my father, but just a cousin with the same name.

My hopes were raised again. My father was alive and, although they hadn't seen him for some time, they hadn't heard that he was dead. My father was a Romany, it transpired. Rose assured me she would try to help find him, so we'd keep in touch. What more could I ask?

Hope was alive and kicking, and I felt that all I had to do was wait. That wouldn't cause any problems. I'd been waiting all of my life.

SEVEN

My reputation as a psychic had followed me; from time to time, I would help where I could. Not necessarily providing life after death, but my 'voice' always providing the right answers to problems.

The fact that I was able to tell the problem without any prior information was astonishing in itself. Many times I would test myself, sitting on a bus or in a cafe; I would tune in to someone I didn't know and be able to see into their lives. On occasions, I would be urged to approach the person concerned and found that these souls had desperately needed someone to talk to and therefore felt better after our chats.

Daisy was one of these souls; she broke down and cried. She was having a tough time at home. Her mother was very possessive of her - loved her too much, perhaps - and wouldn't hear of her marrying the boy she loved.

"Was your mother like that with you?" she asked.

"No, love, not quite," I replied softly.

"Well, you couldn't possibly understand, if your mother was never cruel towards you."

"Perhaps not, Daisy, but I'm a good listener," was all I said.

She invited me to her home and, after many close chats with her mother, Daisy married the love of her life, with mother's approval, and emigrated to Canada. Mother went, too.

On Monday the 20th of March, I received a letter from Mum telling me that Ronnie was putting John into Welfare care, and suggesting I should move back home so she could look after John while I went to work. There was no hesitation, I was going to see my baby. This time we would stay together.

Mick was upset at my decision. "Why don't you bring him down here," he suggested. "And when your divorce comes through, we could get married and I'll look after him."

"But I don't love you, Mick," I murmured.

"Well let me worry about that, we've got plenty of time," he said.

So it was that we arrived at the Childrens' Home in Edinburgh. John hadn't been there an hour. I took him out. Mum had suggested that we go to Fife for a few days and, although I felt anxious as we drove into the town, I was pleased to see her and she was pleased to see me.

We stayed a few days then headed down south. I found out that Ronnie's girl friend hadn't accepted John, so he'd been staying with a sister-in-law. He seemed cheerful enough and soon settled into life in Margate.

I had contacted the local hospital again, only to be told that Matron was away and that the deputy Matron could not employ anyone. However, they would be in touch. So I continued cashiering at the food market.

Tuesday afternoons I had off, so some friends and I would don our bikinis and enter the weekly beauty competition, held at the Margate Lido. The prizes were very good. You could win lamps, bathroom scales, stockings – all sorts of things. So, every Tuesday would find me arriving home with a prize. We certainly didn't enter because we thought we were terrific; the prizes were the main attraction, and we got our photographs in the local papers.

At weekends, I entered talent competitions, in which I usually did well. A Jewish gentleman had approached me and asked if I would consider joining his little troupe of entertainers, visiting convalescent homes to sing for the residents and cheer them up. It was all voluntary work, and I readily agreed; after all, I had done this in my beloved Dunoon.

We all had a great time, helping people on the road to recovery, and I always supplied little bits from the spirit side, too, and found it helped tremendously.

Sunday night was talent night at the Winter Gardens. You auditioned in the afternoon and, if you were lucky, you got through. The first time I went for the audition, I was nervous; it all seemed so professional. There were some marvellous singers, who all handed their music to Bert Hayes, the band leader who did Crackerjack on BBC-TV. Of course, I didn't have any music. I didn't realise it was so serious!

My name was called, and up I went.

"Got your music?" he asked.

"No, didn't know I'd need any."

One raised eyebrow looked up at me. "What ya gonna sing?"

I gulped, and blurted out, "Your Cheating Heart."

"What key?"

"I don't know," wishing I'd stayed away.

With a sigh of discontent he told me to go to the microphone and start. So I did.

Half way through the song he stopped me. "OK, that's fine, thank you."

Stepping off-stage without looking at him, I headed for the door as he called the next one up. Golly, I didn't like that, that was a trial!

Mine host of these Sunday evenings was Gordon Turner, and he called after me. "Be here at six o'clock and no later."

I'd passed the audition.

I arrived back at six with a long evening dress, hung it up in the dressing-room and joined everyone back at the table until I was told to get ready. There were John, Mick, some of his family and some friends, and they were all excited for me. The atmosphere was electric.

By the time I arrived on-stage, my legs were shaking; I was so glad I'd got a long dress on. I received a good ovation when I'd finished. I did manage to win third place, so I was more than pleased, but I decided there and then that show business was definitely not for me. It was too nerve-wracking. I didn't mind singing, but this was something else. Still, we never missed a Sunday show.

Living in Margate was like being on holiday all the time. A friend, with whom I did the local beauty competitions, had become Miss Margate 1967, and called round for us to go and watch the choosing of Miss Cliftonville. On arrival at the hotel, she told me that I had been entered. Although I was tidily dressed, I was certainly not dressed for such an occasion!

All the local dignitaries were there, and the girls all looked their best. The place was crowded.

"Come on," said Sue. "Don't be a spoil-sport, you

stand a good chance of winning. Anyhow, it's a laugh!"

So, off I went backstage, and was given a number. We were called one by one to walk around the stage, then we were interviewed. Then, backstage to await the result. I had already picked a girl I was sure would win. The drums rolled, and the second runner-up was called out, then the first.

I was chatting away to one of the girls, while looking toward the one whom I felt would be called now, and I didn't even hear my name mentioned until I was literally pushed on-stage. I couldn't believe it, I was the new Miss Cliftonville of 1967.

No one was more surprised than me. After that, it was champagne, flowers and presents, and a cash prize of five guineas. Mick and his pals had arrived after the event, and they were as pleased as punch when they discovered what had happened.

Margaret had stayed at home to wash her hair and watch TV. John was in bed. When we got home, I ran upstairs and woke him up, and we all danced round the room. I would be visiting all the towns in Kent, representing Cliftonville. I couldn't sleep – we were all so excited.

The following Tuesday, the 23rd of May, I was splashed all over the papers: 'SCOTS LASS WINS BEAUTY TITLE'. So began a fabulous year, in more ways than one.

A month later, Rose wrote to say she'd heard that my father was in Wishaw in Lanarkshire, so perhaps the local police could help once more. The chase was on again and, on the 9th of July 1967, I received the following letter:

Dear Madam,
I refer to your letter regarding the whereabouts of your father, Mr Peter Mcguigan, and have to inform you that a man by the name of Peter McGuigan resided in the Wishaw area until a few weeks ago. He left, supposedly, to go to Carnworth, Lanarkshire, but the police have found no trace of such a person. However further enquiries will be made and if any information comes to hand I will inform you.
Yours faithfully, The Chief Constable.

Well, this was becoming no easy task and, although I knew I was getting warmer, I told myself that my dream had been lost once, so take it as it comes.

Carrying out my 'Miss Cliftonville' duties, I was invited to the Winter Gardens to Roy Hudd's Summer Show, named 'Hudd's Here'. Guests included Mark Winter, pop star. Roy presented me with a beautiful bouquet, and then I was escorted to a club to have dinner and drinks with the stars.

Whilst chatting to Roy Hudd, I could see a man in spirit with him. When I asked him who he was, he said, "Me name's Miller, love."

Since then, Roy has been aware of the great Max Miller and carries on his work today, much to the delight of Mr Miller.

Of course, Mark Winter was the heart-throb of the sixties; all the girls loved him, and I was no exception. I still have the mementoes of the evening spent in their company.

During August, I received an invitation to Frank's wedding and, in the same post, I was informed that my divorce hearing would be in the High Court in

Edinburgh on 23rd of February 1968. Memories flooded back as a shiver ran through me. I didn't know which occasion would be worse, my divorce or meeting all the family together after so many years.

Mum's sister, Maggie, was flying in from New York. I didn't like her. Having worked in London for some years and looking after people like Burt Lancaster, then travelling and working on cruise ships before finally settling in America to work as a maid to a Scots-born American millionairess, she would return every year for a month or so and stay at our house.

During these visits, we would always gather round to see what presents we would receive from her. Our cousin Wilma, who was a little older than myself, was always given more presents than I was. Maggie would fuss her, trying on Yankee dresses, shoes and coats and taking photographs of her all the time, while I stood there wondering why she liked Wilma more than me.

On one of these occasions during my childhood, I was handed a musical box as a present. It was all different shades of wood and played the Elizabethan Serenade; it was a beautiful musical box. I thanked her, then sat on the couch and wound it up. "Margaret, close that box a minute, Wilma can't hear her tune properly."

Looking up, I saw Wilma standing there holding the most beautiful musical box I had ever seen. It was in the shape of a grand piano, and the lid lifted to expose mirrors all round, with a ballerina all dressed in pink, pirouetting.

I looked at mine and said, cheekily, "Why do I always get the worst looking thing?"

With that, Mum lunged at me, snatching the box from me and breaking it as she did so. Belting me across the face, she called me an ungrateful bitch, and sent me to bed. The musical box was confiscated and, although I was never given it back, I found it some years later. It was still broken. I did get my own back on Wilma at school, where I used to knock hell out of her at playtime. Of course, this didn't help any as I was not only belted but Auntie Maggie gave me a hard time as well.

By now, another Christmas was drawing near and, while attending a dinner at Butlins in my capacity as Queen, I was pleased to meet my old friends, Len Abedge and his trio. They were going to Germany to entertain the troops and Len tried, unsuccessfully, to talk me into joining them. We laughed and joked about the great times we'd had, and we were sad to part company.

Before I knew it, February had arrived and off went Margaret, John and I to Edinburgh, where Mum and Dad met us.

I was given a decree absolute by the High Court Judge. Walking down Edinburgh's Golden Mile, I felt so good. We stayed at Mum's, and Mick joined us the following week to attend Frank's wedding; I wondered what I'd been worried about. Mum and Maggie chatted to me in a fashion I'd never experienced before. I was now twenty-six years old and, for the first time, they made me feel like an adult. Mum and I were becoming friends. The wedding went well and Mum didn't once put me down.

Mick, John and I travelled back to Kent. I felt now that I had broken down the barriers at home; my relationship with Esther Hutchison was just beginning and, although it had taken over twenty-four years, to me it was better late than never.

On our arrival back in Margate on the 23rd of March, my final divorce papers were waiting. I was legally single. Mick took no time in, once again, asking me to marry him. As I had been granted a decree absolute, I could remarry straight away. The following Saturday, March the 30th 1968, Mick and I were married; Margaret was maid of honour. I was a bundle of nerves as I dressed. Taking off Ronnie's wedding ring, along with the garnet birth-stone ring I had always worn, doubt began to fill my mind. Was I doing the right thing? Would Mick change as Ronnie had, once I was legally his?

"Come on, now," Margaret said, interrupting my thoughts. "You'll be all right, Mick's OK."

Mick's mum and sisters had arranged a buffet at home. John hadn't wanted to come to the wedding, as he had begun roller-skating at Margate's Dreamland and much preferred to go there.

Since we hadn't planned any more than the wedding, we spent the evening at a dance to choose the local beauty queen of Westbrook.

On Mick's suggestion that I enter, I was chosen maid of honour. My own crown would have to be given up soon as my year was almost finished, so it was nice to know that I'd be able to travel for another year. The following week's headlines in the paper read: BRIDE IN THE MORNING, MAID OF HONOUR IN THE EVENING.

We arrived home after a fairly full day, emotionally speaking, and, on retiring, I went to the dressing-table to put away Ronnie's wedding ring. It had gone. Mick denied seeing it; in fact, no one had seen it. I became very upset, for that ring had not left my finger since 1960. I knew I had left it there with the garnet ring, which hadn't moved, but we searched everywhere with no luck. The next time I was to see this token of love from Ronnie was to be in 1986, nine years after his death, given back to me by him from the world of spirit.

Mick, John and I moved into a nice flat in Cliftonville. Unfortunately, our dear little budgie, Charlie, couldn't join us, as he had died a few weeks before.

Margaret took herself a flat not too far away, was still courting Colin, and they planned to marry soon. Colin, like Margaret's first husband, was in the Navy, so was away a lot of the time.

I was accepted at the district hospital as an auxiliary nurse. Stating that I would prefer to work nights, I began training through the day and eventually moved onto night duty. Each night found me on a different ward, and I loved every minute of it. I always knew when a patient needed me, just as I knew when one was ready to pass over to the spirit side. And I always gave what comfort I could.

Mrs Baxter was one such patient; she insisted on rising each morning to make the tea and take it round. Always cheerful, this very sick lady never thought of herself. I would tell her to stay in bed and let one of the other ladies do the morning tea.

"No, no, nurse, the other ladies are here to rest; they have to go home and look after their families. It doesn't matter about me. I'll be resting long enough. So please let me fuss them, it makes me feel useful," she said.

"You shouldn't talk like that," I chided her. "You'll be going home soon."

She was suffering from radium sickness; unfortunately, radium therapy is a treatment that can kill. We would sit in the middle of the night with a cuppa, chatting about everything under the sun.

"Do you believe in an after-life," she asked one night. "Yes, very much so," I said.

"And what makes you so confident?"

I began to speak of my spirit friends and my 'voice', and she listened intently.

"Who do you think this man is, that you hear?"

"He's my spirit guide; he helps people by telling me what to say to them."

"Can he cure people who are dying?" she asked.

"No, he can't stop anyone from dying if it is their time. We all have a time to live and a time to die. There are, however, a lot of illnesses that can be cured from the spirit side. But we never die, we cannot, we just move on spiritually, we go back home. My guide says that no one here can stop the law of human nature. He believes that ninety-five per cent of illness is in the mind. The other five per cent is of a physical nature."

"He sounds very wise, this guide of yours."

"Yes, he is," I told her.

"Does he have a name?"

"No, I've asked but he doesn't say."

"Where does he come from?"

"I don't know, he's just there."

"Doesn't he frighten you?"

"Oh no, he never frightens me, I love him."

"What religion is he?" she asked.

"He isn't any religion, he says religion is man-made and not of God as we know him."

"Are you religious, nurse?"

"No, I'm not religious, but I do believe there is a power over all of us and I do believe that we should be given the freedom of choice as regards religion, and not have it forced on us when we are young. This is indoctrination and I don't believe in it. It causes conflict between different beliefs and traditions, just like colour does. To me, it doesn't matter what your colour is, or your creed, it's what's inside that counts. Orthodox religions leave too much doubt as to whether there really is a life hereafter. We are trying to come to terms with something that has been practised by Eastern religions for centuries. That the soul lives on. We cannot die."

"You are a very wise young lady, nurse. You have made me feel so much better," and she leaned over and kissed me on the cheek. "God bless you, love," she said and crept off to bed.

Walking home through the park that morning, I felt uneasy in my stomach over Mrs Baxter.

After getting John off to school, I told Mick of my feelings and he told me to stop being stupid. He worked nights down the pit, so we would usually have breakfast together and then go to bed.

That morning was the start of my three days off, so I wasn't due on duty until the Friday night. I only slept for a few hours, as I would be in bed that night, so I got up and started my chores. Periodically, Mrs Baxter would come to mind and the strange feeling in my stomach would get stronger. I was restless all that night.

Mick arrived home the next morning to find me in tears. "What's wrong love?"

"It's Mrs Baxter, I didn't say goodbye."

"Oh, I'm sorry," he said. "When did you find out she'd died?"

"I haven't found out, Mick, I just know."

"Oh, come on now, she's probably all right, you're just worried."

"No, I've got that feeling in my stomach; I always get it when somebody's dying."

"Well, why don't you pop up to the hospital to see her, to put your mind at rest?"

"Yes, I'll do that," I said.

I tried to put it out of my mind and went for a game of Bingo that afternoon. From there, I walked up to the hospital and chatted to some of the nurses.

On the pretence that I'd left my book on the ward, I headed in. The curtains were drawn around Mrs Baxter's bed. Drawing them aside, tears filled my eyes; she had passed away, and looked so peaceful.

Her husband had already visited and had placed a single red rose in her hands, which were crossed over her chest. I spent a few minutes with her, then gently kissed her on the forehead. She was now at her rest. She had passed a few hours before.

My strange stomach had ceased. This was a feeling of which I had become aware some time before, and have often been aware of since. I cried all the way home and Mick got mad at me, saying I'd have to learn to be harder. It was no good being soft when dealing with death every day. Besides, he added, why should I, so certain that you lived when you died, get so upset?

That remark was like a slap in the face, and I shouted at him for not having any compassion.
He just shrugged his shoulders and walked off.

EIGHT

Because of staff shortages, I was placed indefinitely on a male ward, where I found men to be better patients than women. They may have acted like babies at home, when they were poorly, but they became first-class patients in hospital. We did have some laughs, when I would try to hide my embarrassment at some of the remarks, but I soon learned to hold my own with them.

After a few months, I was back on the other wards, much to the dismay of my male patients, nearly all of whom had told me that, if they were going to die, they wanted to die in my arms. They were a soppy lot, but I loved them dearly.

I had gone on the Pill, so that we could save up and hopefully buy a house. It was the first time I had ever used a contraceptive and it wasn't agreeing with me. I began to have migraine headaches, my legs were heavy and sore, and I was becoming very depressed. I kept ignoring it, telling myself it was nothing.

One night on the women's ward, there were just two student nurses and myself; the hospital was a training hospital. We had a ward full of patients and the students had gone to the canteen for their break.

Within half an hour, one woman had died and, on my way to phone Night Sister, another took a coronary. My first reaction was to jump on the woman's chest and thump, thump, thump. I felt helpless; there was no one around and I didn't want to panic the other patients. I just carried on and, luckily, she began breathing again.

Doing what I had to do, I phoned the Sister and she came straight away. I suddenly felt so bad. Sister was yelling at me, "Get this. Do that. Nurse, why aren't you more organized?"

That was it. I calmly walked through the door just as the student nurses were coming back from their break.

"Go help Sister," I said, and headed for the changing room.

As I was shaking my hair from my cap, Sister walked in.

"Where do you think you're going?" she enquired.

"I'm going home – I've had enough of your bossing." All the nurses were afraid of this particular Sister, who was very domineering, but a first-class nurse, and nobody, but nobody, ever answered her back.

"Let's talk about it," she said.

I broke down crying. She put her arm around my shoulders and suggested I should go and see my doctor, first thing in the morning.

"I'm so sorry for taking my feelings out on you," I said.

"That's OK. Now, don't worry, you go and have a few hours sleep in the rest room."

At the surgery next morning, my doctor told me I had to stop the Pill, which was the cause of my headaches. Too much oestrogen. He told me I was very lucky; a few more pills, and I probably would have dropped dead with a thrombosis. The Pill, in the late sixties, claimed a lot of lives, and I had almost become a victim myself.

Back on the ward that night, Sister took me aside. After I had told her of my visit to the doctor, she quietly said, "Do you know, you probably saved that patient's life last night."

Looking towards the patient, I smiled. As I walked towards the bed, Sister called out, "Nurse, mind you, you broke one of her ribs doing it! A small price to pay, though, don't you think?"

There was a twinkle in her eye as she walked off. I felt better already.

I was sent on the private ward for a time. This was for paying patients, who could afford the treatment, and these women seemed to think that you had to appear in front of them as soon as they rang.

I called them the 'Silver Spoon Brigade'. Some were very nice, but the majority were a really unhappy lot. They had acquired things too easily in life and their idea of security didn't stem beyond their bank balance. Although they thought they did, they didn't actually receive any better treatment than that given to NHS patients. They did, however, have silver service bestowed on them, similar to a hotel. I felt sad for these people; class distinction is a terrible thing.

Sitting in the office one night, I could hear someone shuffling up the corridor but, on checking, I found everyone tucked up safely in bed. Thinking it must have been my imagination, I carried on with my paperwork. I heard it again and, this time, the footsteps seemed to be shuffling towards the office door. I looked up, expecting one of the patients to appear; no one did, but the shuffling ceased.

"Yes?" I called out. There was no reply.

Up I got again and just caught sight of a woman going into the room at the far end of the corridor. What on earth's she doing, I thought, that's Mr Law's room. So I hurried down, only to find Mr Law fast asleep and the lady nowhere to be seen.

Checking out his room, I was puzzled. I investigated all the other rooms, but everyone was accounted for. I knew she couldn't have wandered through the main doors, into the ward, as the office was right next to the door.

I phoned the night porter and asked him to call in. When I had explained what had happened, he told me I had just met the nun, who was known to haunt the ward. The private ward was part of the original building and, although I never did check the story, it appeared that some people had seen her in the past, but she had only ever been seen entering that one particular room, which might have been a chapel many years previously.

That morning, arriving home, I picked up the mail. The postmark on one of the letters set me off. It was from Lanarkshire. I ripped it open; it was from my father!

When I had made my enquiry, I had enclosed a photograph of myself and had asked the police if they would please pass it on should they find him. I felt so sick with joy that I couldn't read it straight away.

In his letter, my father explained to me how my mother would not marry him, and how much he'd loved her. Shortly after I'd been born, they'd had an argument and split up, whereupon I stayed with him and his mother. He came home from work, one day, to find that my mother had come and taken me away.

So, my father carried on travelling the country and then lost touch. He wanted me to believe how he was always thinking about me. He had entered the Army but couldn't settle, and was now married to another Romany and hoped I wouldn't think any the less of him. He explained how it had all happened during the war years, and how the world had been upside down. Everyone had been very uncertain as to what the future held.

I read, and reread, the letter and sat down to answer it, telling him where I had been brought up and all about his grandson, omitting to mention anything upsetting. I also refrained from mentioning that I was pregnant. I hadn't told anyone at the hospital, either, until one morning, as I came off duty, Matron asked to see me in her office. I was six months, but it didn't show.

When she asked me if it was true that I was pregnant, I had to tell her. She was horrified to think that I had been working twelve hours a night, lifting heavy patients, and had no alternative but to ask me to stop straight away, pointing out that the hospital could get into trouble if anything happened to me. I was very upset at having to go, but I had no choice.

Michelle was born on the 26th of July 1969, and John was over the moon at having a little sister. He was now eight. Mum came down straight away from Fife; I was a little bit anxious, remembering what had happened when John was born, but she was all right. She had come to stay for two weeks, and I decided not to mention anything about my father.

One of Mick's friends was at the flat one night,

when the discussion turned to ouija boards. Mum suggested we set one up, so we did; it began moving straight away. We asked silly questions. I was afraid of it and told Mum we shouldn't use it, but she was enjoying herself.

"What's going to win the two o'clock at Lingfield tomorrow?" and it spelled out a name. The next day, Mick's mate put a few shillings on it. It won. So, out the ouija board came again that night, and the questions got more serious.

I suggested we stop. My 'voice' then said, "Don't dabble, you're attracting low-level entities."

So I refused to play it again. Later, when only Mum and I were sitting in the flat, she started telling me about her mother, whom she had idolized. As she was talking, I could see the lady appear behind her, the same lady I had seen in our parlour all those years before. I had obviously never known her, and had never seen a picture of her.

I began to tell Mum, who asked, "What does she look like?"

So I described her. When I said, "She wore a shiny brooch on her shawl," Mum went pale.

"That's my mother, all right," she gasped. "I put that brooch on her myself, before we closed her coffin."

We talked into the small hours. Each spirit visitor I remembered seeing when I was young, my mother had known. She then confided in me that, when I was small, she had known I was different. How I would talk in my sleep when we lived in the pit-row, coming out with a vocabulary of words even she didn't understand, and holding conversations with unseen people.

She told me how she would listen for someone else's voice, but could only hear mine answering. She told me how frightened she had been, as she couldn't understand, and how Dad used to tell her to stop fussing and just ignore it.

"Was this why you used to hit me so much?" I asked.

"Yes, I didn't know what else to do; I thought I could knock it out of you."

I laughed. "Didn't have much luck, did you?"

"No," she replied.

I asked if this was why Auntie Maggie didn't like me, either.

"Oh, Maggie has never disliked you. What made you think that?"

"Well, Wilma always got the special treatment from her."

Mum then told me how Maggie was really Wilma's mother, not her aunt. When Maggie had decided to leave the area, after being let down by the father, Auntie Teeny had taken Wilma in and brought her up as her own. Wilma was the only reason Maggie returned periodically. I began, at last, to understand.

We were sitting having a cup of tea in a cafe in Margate when a lady sitting opposite suddenly took a fit of coughing. She was vainly fumbling for her handkerchief in her bag, so Mum took hers out and handed it to the woman.

"It's not funny when your tea goes down your throat, is it?"

"No, it's not," replied the woman, her voice all husky. When she'd calmed down, she thanked Mum and they began chatting. Mum commented on the woman's sore throat, to be told that she'd spoken like that since she'd been operated on for cancer of the larynx. I sat feeding Michelle while they blathered.

"My name is Mrs Wedgewood, love."

Mum extended her hand. "Mrs Hutchison, dear, pleased to meet you, and this is my daughter."

I felt strange, hearing her say that. Mrs Wedgewood then proceeded to tell Mum how she'd shed many tears, mentioning instances Mum easily related to.

Turning to me, Mrs Wedgewood said, "You've suffered a lot, too, haven't you dear?"

"Well, a bit," I replied sheepishly.

"You must understand, it's for a reason. I am a medium, and so are you. You're here to do God's work, just as I am, and it's not an easy path, as you may well know. But you'll make it."

"Thank you," I answered.

We were sorry to leave this lady, she was so interesting. Mum said, "You know something funny, Margaret? I always seem to at attract mediums – I must be psychic!"

She sounded very proud of that statement, and I began to laugh.

When I saw her off on the coach at the end of her stay, Mum kissed me on the cheek, promising to come again soon. Tears filled my eyes as I watched her waving cheerily. Putting my hand up to my cheek, I told myself I wasn't going to wash my face for a week. After all those years, Esther Hutchison had finally accepted me.

We moved to just outside Margate. A few months later, I was walking to the shop when I thought I recognized the woman walking toward me. It was

Mrs Wedgewood. She remembered me too.

"I knew I'd meet you again, love," she said.

It turned out she lived only a few doors round the corner from me. So began our friendship and, as it would turn out, our work together.

Millie had come from Lancashire and, through marriage, was a member of the famous Wedgewood family. She told us how her father was in the Salvation Army, while Millie leaned towards spiritualism. Of how, on arriving home one evening, she had watched her father fall into a trance as he sat by the fire, a lad's voice coming through passing a message to be taken to his relative who lived some distance away.

Millie had hurriedly written the message down as, on her father's awakening, he had no recollection of the event and would have nothing to do with the taking of a message from a discarnate. So, Millie had taken the message herself, walking most of the way, finally arriving at the address to find the family in mourning for their son. He had been killed in a freak accident only a few days before. The family accepted the evidence she supplied.

Her father had eventually become a spiritualist too. I asked her how she had put it to the family.

"Straight out love, straight out. It was the only way."

Millie was of the old school, and had sat in circles with Gordon Higginson's mother and had watched him grow up into spiritualism. A well-known medium called Nan Mackenzie was also a personal friend, as was Harry Edwards, Healer Extraordinaire.

Each morning would find Millie and me eating toast, drinking tea and chatting. I had confided in her about my father and how, although we were still writing to each other, we'd been unable to arrange a meeting. I was troubled about this, as he'd given me a phone box number to phone on Thursday the 20th of December at 8 p.m. The number just rang and rang and, after an hour of constant trying, I had given up and hadn't heard from him since.

What was wrong? I didn't know, so one morning, over our tea and toast, I asked Millie if she would give me a reading.

She began, firstly, to inform me that my spirit guide was Chinese and around two hundred years old; his name, she said, would be given to me in different circumstances, and the next ten years would hold many tears for me, but also some joys. I was never to deny the spirit side, even when the going got rough.

She said, "Always remember, when the going gets tough, the tough get going."

It was the first time that I'd heard that phrase.

Another child is on its way, she told me. I was, in fact, pregnant as she spoke and didn't know.

"I'm getting strong Australian connections around your mother, is she there?"

"I don't know where she is."

"Haven't you tried to find her?"

"Yes, when I was eighteen I went to Glasgow and all they could give me was the address of the lady who had taken me to them, but the whole street had been pulled down some years before."

"Well, love," she said, "you will find out where she is, but don't expect too much, will you?"

"All right," I whispered, amazed at what she'd said already.

My doctor confirmed my pregnancy and I wasn't too happy about it, as I had not intended having any more children, but, of course, now I had no choice.

I wasn't seeing much of Mick. He worked all day Monday to Friday, and then was out all day Saturday and Sunday working on cars or boats. He'd also taken a job on Friday and Saturday nights as a bouncer in a night-club, and was drinking a lot.

I kept myself busy painting and decorating, which I did rather enjoy, and then there were all the piles of washing and ironing to do. This was hard work, as I didn't own a washing-machine.

Thinking about my father, my strange stomach would play up.

All our furniture was on credit, and I found I was robbing Peter to pay Paul, most weeks. I'd go and play Bingo with a neighbour, Nan, a dear lady who became my second mother and still is. It was during one of these visits that my psychic gifts were brought up. After that, I found that the interval was taken up giving readings in the ladies toilets.

I went into labour while playing Bingo. Everyone was concerned except me! I was determined to finish my few leisure hours as I would be confined for ten days when the baby arrived; I had begged my doctor to let me have this one at home, but he flatly refused. Because of my small feet, he told me.

Refusing offers of a lift home, because Mick was picking me up, I waited in the freezing cold. The labour pains were coming rapidly. Rain lashed down for what seemed an eternity. The Bingo Hall was on the rocks on the seashore and the sea was rushing up over the prom. It was a beautiful place in the summer, but could be very bleak in winter.

I ended up fighting my way home through the wind and rain, my contractions coming every few minutes. When I got indoors, I found that Mick hadn't come home from the pub. I phoned everyone I could think of in Margate and left a message at each place. He finally arrived home at midnight and took me to the hospital.

Lee was born at 3.45 am. It was the 28th of October, 1970.

Mum had not been able to leave Dad as he wasn't keeping too well. The doctors had told Mum that he would possibly have ten years left with only one lung; this lung was now labouring. In my letters to her, I would tell her how well things were with us, even though we were struggling more than ever.

I couldn't afford to buy new clothes, so a neighbour convinced me that jumble sales offered a variety of good clothes. So it was. All our best clothes came from them. I enjoyed jumbling; bargains could be found for next to nothing.

Fortunately, I was good at cooking, so I would bake a lot and make stews; buying tinned food was out, because I couldn't afford it. Some weeks, Mother Hubbard would not have had a look in!

However, I always did manage Millie's toast each morning, but recall one occasion when I got up and found that the only two slices of bread I had had were gone. One of the kids had been hungry and had eaten them. I sent John round to the neighbours to borrow a few slices, but he couldn't get an answer.

I was so worried about Millie's toast, so I thought I would tell her that I would have to go to the shop for some, and would ask to have the bread on credit, as I could not pay for it.

On opening the door, however, there stood Millie, a fresh loaf in her hand. "I thought it was time I supplied the bread," she whispered. She knew how hard up I was. Of course, I wasn't the only one. A lot of my friends and neighbours were in the same boat and we would help each other out as best we could.

I had been so stupid to allow myself to get pregnant. However, for the time being, I would have to make the best of the situation.

NINE

Recognizing neither the hand-writing, nor the postmark, on the envelope in the post, I began to read the letter contained therein. My real father, Peter McGuigan, had had a heart attack and died.

I just broke down and cried. That was why I hadn't got his call. I was devastated. So near we were, yet it was not to be. Once again, reality had intervened. A reality I had brought upon myself. I wiped my eyes, no more tears now. I promised myself that I would never allow anything to upset me so much again. Determination to find my real mother took over, and I became a very protective mother towards my children. I would never allow anyone to look after them. I couldn't bring myself to trust anyone, anyway, not after my own childhood.

John was always helpful with the babies, and around the house. Mick loved them to death and, as they grew older, I made sure that he looked after them too. It was very important to me to keep this marriage together.

I would never have been able to cope with three children alone, so I tended to ignore the problems we were having. All too often, women like myself find themselves trapped in an unhappy situation for the sake of the kids.

I did love Mick very much, but I didn't see much of his family as they were older and all went to work.

His mother worked days and evenings, so the only time she saw the children was when Mick took them on an occasional Sunday morning. Of course, I had no relatives at all.

Mum had said that Dad felt that he could make the journey down, so they arrived for a holiday. It was 1973, and it was great having them here. They played non-stop with the kids and, of course, Michelle and Lee had never known grandparents before.

Mum was thrilled to see Mrs Wedgewood again and to meet Nan. They got on like a house on fire. I was driving by then; Mick came by cars easily, for his banger racing, and could pick up a decent one for a fiver, so I was able to drive Mum and Dad around the Kent countryside. Dad found the air here most agreeable to him.

His breathing seemed much better and he reckoned that, if he had been younger, he would have moved down here. They did enjoy themselves.

I told Mum about my real dad, and she cried. She told me that Pat had done the same; however, when visiting his mother, he had not revealed his identity because he didn't like her on sight. So that part of his life had now been buried, and Mum felt that any discussion of Frank's roots would not be wise.

"Why didn't you write to the Welfare?" she asked.

"I've already told you of my visit there when I was eighteen."

"Was that your mother's or father's name on your birth certificate?"

I told her it was my father's.

"Well I'd get back to the Welfare if I were you; they must have more information than they told you. I expect that whoever dealt with you just couldn't be bothered to look it up."

So Mum and I sat down and wrote to them. Dad's only comment was that we should let sleeping dogs lie.

"How are things with you and Mick?" Mum asked.

"Oh, fine, we're all right." I said.

She looked at me and said, "Don't ever try to kid a mother, Margaret; we know better."

"Well," I said, "things will get better as the kids get older," and I changed the subject.

I was so sorry to see them go, and wished that they lived nearer. I didn't know when, or if, I'd see them again.

I hadn't been keeping too well and, since having Lee, my doctor had put me on another Pill which contained less oestrogen. I just always felt so tired and, although I had never, ever, hit my kids, I had become very short tempered.

I was put on antidepressants; this was quite alien to me, as I'd never taken tablets before. I felt like an old woman.

On the 4th of August that year I opened a letter from the Glasgow Welfare Department. I began to shake. Sat myself down, and read:

Dear Madam,
I am replying to your letter of the 28th ultimo and have to inform you that, according to our records, you were born on the 6th of January 1942, in Stobhill Hospital, Springburn, Glasgow. Your mother was Mary MacDonald, being unmarried and at that time living at lodgings at 43 London Road, Glasgow. She was born on the

8th of April 1922 in New Sneddan Street, Paisley and her parents are both dead. It would appear from the records that your mother's parents had lived in Paisley for a considerable number of years, up to 1941. The last addresses being given as New Inchinnan Road, Paisley and Cart Lane, Paisley and of course your mother herself was born there. You came into the Corporation's care at the age of about nine months, when you were handed over to the Welfare Department by a Mrs Thompson of George Street, Glasgow, in whose care you had been left by your mother, who was then in desertion and her whereabouts were unknown. There was never any further contact with your mother and I regret being unable to supply you with any further information about her, or any relatives.
Yours faithfully, The Senior Social Worker

I read it over and over again and became angry to think that I could have had this information thirteen years before, if only some silly employee there had taken five minutes to look for it. Well, I'd got it now, so what should I do? I wrote to the Police Department at Paisley to see if they would be able to enlighten me further and, on the 16th of August, I received a reply. My mother was now married and living in Australia.

Australia! It jumped out of the page at me. Milly Wedgewood had been right. "Strong Australian connections with your mother," she had said.

Names and addresses of other relatives, both here and in Scotland, were given. I ran to show Milly the information. She thought for a moment and said, "Don't you think it hurts Mr and Mrs Hutchison to know all this?"

"No I don't. Mum helped me to write the letter to the Welfare."

"I know she did, love, but it still hurt her. She's worried that you might find something more that will distress you. After all, if your real mother had wanted to see you, don't you think she would have done so by now?"

"Yes I suppose you're right, but I'm curious. I've got to know – I've a right to know."

"Of course you have, love, of course you have," was all she said.

I needed to find out everything I could but, at that time, I could not pluck up the courage to contact any of my relatives. It was such a strange feeling. Wanting to contact them but frightened to do so. I finally decided that it would be better if I were able to contact my mother direct, without the help of her relatives.

Perhaps they didn't know about me; after all, she had been an unmarried mother and, if I'd been a cupboard skeleton, I didn't want to shake any old bones – and perhaps her husband had no knowledge of me. I would, however, cross that bridge when I came to it. So, I thought a safe bet would be a letter to my late grandmother's sister whose address had been contained with the others.

The pretence was that I was a friend of Mary's, had lost her address, and could she help? I received a quick reply, saying that she had lost touch after the murder of Mary's mother in Glasgow; obviously assuming that I would know about this, she did not elaborate.

I hadn't expected anything like this and, curiosity

getting the better of me, wrote to the Police Headquarters in Glasgow for more information on this blow that I'd received.

I opened the letter dated the 19th of September 1973, and read how my grandmother had been found murdered, battered to death by a person unknown. The only clue they had found was a footprint of a military-style boot, issued mainly to U.S. and Canadian servicemen; many such servicemen had sailed the very morning she was found. Although extensive enquiries were made, not only in the United Kingdom but also on ships which landed in the U.S. and Canada, the culprit was never found.

A story carried by a newspaper in 1958, regarding this unsolved murder, told of how well-thought-of my grandmother had been by all who knew her. Forty-six years old, and a widow, she had worked hard to bring up a family of seven. So, another part of my family roots had been disclosed.

At Mick's suggestion to leave well alone, I put all this to the back of my mind — for the moment, anyway.

Mick had a new boss at work, Harry, who was interested in psychic matters. During a discussion one evening, Harry said, "Mick reckons you can leave your body. Is that right?"

"Yes, of course — we all can, and do," I replied.

"Well, I've tried and can't do it." As the discussion progressed he decided it was all rubbish and that Astral Travel was not possible.

"OK. Here's what I'll do to prove the point. I have no idea where you live or what your personal circumstances are, but tonight I'll travel to you. Pop in tomorrow and I'll show you how possible it is."

Satisfied with the thought that I'd no more convince him tomorrow than I had today, he went on his way.

Lying in bed that night, I found myself travelling at height. I recall thinking how I hadn't realized that people lived above the pleasure arcades on Margate seafront. I looked through windows, watching people looking at TV, while some drew curtains before retiring.

In a matter of moments I landed in a room. It was a bedroom and there was Harry, face down on a bed, fast asleep. Taking in all that I saw in the room, my eyes moved to one corner, where there was a cot with a baby in it. Whether Harry sensed someone around I don't know, but he began to stir. So I jokingly pulled the bedclothes from him and saw that he was wearing pants, blue in colour, with a lilac band around the waist! Then off I went.

The following afternoon, the two of them arrived. Harry teased me about my promised Astral trip, and Mick just sat there, interested.

I produced a drawing of his bedroom I had made that morning, and Harry's smile began to fade as I showed him where each piece of furniture was placed. I told him about the baby.

Harry sat down, completely stunned, and told us that, when he had arrived home the night before, his landlord had been disappointed at not being able to attend a dinner with his wife, as their babysitter couldn't sit. Harry had suggested moving the baby into his room for the night, as he was staying in, so they had shifted Harry's room around to fit the cot in. When I laughingly told him I had moved his bedclothes, and described the pants he had been wearing, he jumped up and excitedly showed me he was still wearing them. He was totally convinced.

After that episode, I found a stream of people, mostly workmen, wishing a reading from me. A stream which has grown and grown over the years.

My health was still none too good and I found that my 'ladies department' had decided to cause me problems.

After various confinements in hospital to rectify the situation, I found myself unable even to walk. I was getting weaker and losing blood constantly. My doctor, unable to diagnose a condition, would visit me every evening and I renamed him Dracula: always visiting late at night and most times drawing blood from me. He was a wonderful man; he even visited me at weekends and constantly kept me cheerful.

It was during this year of total confinement that I began studying various religions.

I had resigned myself to the fact that I might not recover, a fact that did not cause me any concern. I was lucky; I knew where I'd be going if my time was up here. I'd be going home. I'd see James, and perhaps meet my real father. I'd meet my grandmother for the first time. No, there was certainly no sadness for me at this possibility, and I would still be able to watch my children grow, and help them, from the spirit side.

On many occasions I would find myself in this beautiful land of spirit. Although there is no sun as we know it, it is so bright and warm - radiating love. I was quite looking forward to my return there from this earth, where I had found more tears than joy.

There was no fear of Hell for me. Hell is merely a suggestion inflicted upon us by society, as are many things.

It was around four o'clock one morning that I found myself being put into an ambulance. I heard the doctor tell Mick that I was deteriorating fast and that we would be travelling to the hospital in Herne Bay, where a surgeon would take a look at me. I only remember the coldness of the theatre and voices talking around me.

Sadly, the afternoon of that same day found me back at home in bed. There was no point in wasting a bed on me at the hospital, and they still hadn't determined my condition.

Mum had arrived to help at home and she was very good, but I felt so sorry for giving her this worry. Dad's health had also been declining, so it was a lot for her to cope with. However, she did keep me cheery, telling jokes, and my neighbours, especially Nan, loved her very much and never stopped laughing at the comical things she came out with.

Sitting on my bed one night, Mum said she was going into Margate the following morning and what would I like her to buy me? All the time I hadn't been feeling too great, one thing had kept on niggling me: I felt a desperation to own a new pair of red shiny shoes.

"Red shiny shoes, Mum, that's what I'd like."

"That's a strange thing to ask for, hen," she said.

"Yes," I reflected, "I used to own a pair, but had them confiscated when I tried to run away from the convent. I'd worked very hard for those red shoes, having been given them as payment for work done in the laundry."

With that, Mum looked at me and collapsed in a heap of tears, and then we hugged each other for a few moments.

"I'll buy you the best pair of red shiny shoes that money can buy," she wept.

It was obvious that the family did not believe that I was going to last much longer, and my brother Frank and his wife travelled down to visit me, as did Auntie Maggie. It was nice to see them; I hadn't seen Frank since his wedding in 1968 which, of course, had been my wedding year too. Shortly after they all returned to Scotland, I woke up one morning and felt great. I couldn't believe it; I wasn't bleeding any more. I was alone in the house, and felt so strong.

I got out of my bed, which had been built up with bricks at one end so that my feet would be elevated. I couldn't even feel the pain in my back, which had been so bad and constant; I had lain on one side for almost a year because of this pain. I felt newly born.

Unsteadily, I walked into the bathroom, a feat that I'd been unable to accomplish for a very long time. I heard the front door opening downstairs, a few friends arriving; I never locked my doors, so that friends and neighbours always had access.

I called down, proudly announcing that I was coming downstairs. Heading along the landing, I collapsed, haemorrhaging badly.

My friends came running up the stairs and the husband carried me back to my room and phoned the doctor. I was admitted to hospital once again, so mad at myself. This thing wasn't going to beat me. I'd had enough.

My doctor sat on the hospital bed and explained

what they were going to do; they had decided to remove my womb and cervix.

"Thank God for that," I said. "Why couldn't you have taken it out last year?"

He explained to me that they hadn't known for certain where the problem lay and also, because of the continuous bleeding, they hadn't been able to see properly. They had also felt that, at thirty-three, I was a bit young to have a hysterectomy. He told me he would be with me throughout, as he was going to be my anaesthetist; I knew he was worried because I was so frail. He was not only my doctor, but had become my friend, and the last thing I saw before undergoing surgery was his kindly face.

I found myself speeding through a tunnel, which ended in a complete mass of light all round. I knew where I was. There were smiling faces all around and I felt terrific. I saw the outline of a man standing before me. He, too, was smiling. I gazed into his eyes; they mesmerized me, they were so beautiful. I was full of love for this man, and moved closer to him, stretching out my hand for him to take it.

I suddenly woke up, screaming, having never before experienced such pain. Sadly, I was back in my body.

I remained in a poor state, having succumbed to anaesthetic sickness, and was moved to a private room; for a few days, only the family were allowed to visit. I was so weak that they had to bring the X-ray equipment to my room.

Even if the family had doubts about my survival, I had none. My mission was not yet over and, after a few weeks, I began to recover and was taken to another hospital to recuperate. Although I was still in a wheel-chair, my strength was gradually beginning to return.

After I had convinced the hospital doctor that I would take things easy, he let me go home. It was difficult learning to walk again; I would get so mad at myself, and would crawl around on all fours, especially after Mick almost dropped me while carrying me downstairs!

Only three months after my operation, I found myself a job. I felt I'd wasted enough time being sick and, although my doctor reckoned it was too soon, I felt that the sooner I found myself more to think about, the better.

TEN

A two-minute walk from the house was the golf course, situated on which was a nursing home for the elderly where I had applied for a job as a care assistant.

Mrs Elias was the Matron. She was a tiny wee thing, all of four foot ten, but when she spoke everyone certainly took notice. She had come out of retirement at the age of sixty-four to resume her place in this, her nursing home, which she had bought many years before but which, for some years, had been rented out.

Matron told me we would be working hard, as all the beds and furniture were being replaced. When I told her how I really shouldn't be lifting too much weight so soon after my op, she pooh-poohed me and said, "Illness is all in the mind; you must think positively. The mind controls the body, and not vice versa."

I looked at this little soul, and decided we were going to get on fine. She was a Christian Scientist, and I soon became learned in her beliefs, visiting healing sessions and lectures whenever I could. But for me, like other religions, something was missing.

Mary Baker Eddy, founder of the Christian Scientist Movement, had formerly been a Spiritualist and I marvelled at the mind-energy of this woman, who had adopted such a positive attitude towards illness.

Penelope was Mrs Elias's adopted daughter and was the cook, while her husband was general handyman. Penny and I became very close friends, which we remain to this day.

Mrs Elias made me deputy Matron and I soon found myself running the home, while she jaunted off around the world. At one point, she was struck down by meningitis and refused any medical help. Armed only with her Bible and a healer from her church, she warned Penny that, no matter how ill she became, no doctor was to touch her, telling Penny that she would never be forgiven if she allowed this to happen. I felt so sorry for Penny, but reckoned her mother was just being stubborn and, of course, I knew that she had to respect her mother's wishes.

Mrs Elias soon recovered, without any medical aid. The local doctors attending the residence had been only too aware of the fact that Mrs Elias would not entertain them for herself, but would readily call them out if anyone else needed medical attention.

I had become interested in Healing but I couldn't do it, much as I tried, until one evening, early in 1976. Nan and I were having our game of Bingo, when one of the women asked me to give her some healing.

Janet had been having severe head pains, and told me it was a tumour. She needed to have an operation, but the doctors refused to do this as she was not only overweight, but her chest was very wheezy.

Perhaps I wouldn't be able to help, but I was definitely going to try. So, during the interval, off we went to the 'ladies', and I felt all I had to do was stand behind her, with my hands on her head. Within minutes, a great heat was flowing through my fingertips, and I left my hands there until the heat cooled and Janet had fallen asleep. I remained there with her.

When I had removed my hands, I had been soaking wet; my hands and face had been dripping. On awakening, Janet remarked how warm she felt.

Waking up next morning, I couldn't move; my head was spinning and I was wheezing. I hadn't thrown her illness from me. Mick was very annoyed, for I was ill in bed for three days.

On next seeing Janet, she told me that she'd never felt so good in a long time: her headache had stopped that night, as had the wheezing. Now, fourteen years on, she has never had a recurrence.

When she kept her next appointment at the hospital, Janet told the doctor what had happened. It turned out that three of the doctors were interested in meeting me, to find out how I did it, although I hadn't a clue. I arranged to meet them one afternoon; we had a terrific discussion and they all asked me for readings.

The mother of one of the doctors had the same inoperable complaint as Janet and I was asked if I might do healing on her. I eventually did – happily, with the same results.

This time I was fine. I had put in a word upstairs, to take any pain from me, and the spirit side had obliged. I knew then that our work was a two-way contract. Without me, my spirit friends and my guide could do nothing. Without them, neither could I. We were a partnership.

Although Mick always said he was sceptical, he would wake up some nights and tell me to ask the spirit people to shut up, and had they no consideration as he had to get up for work? So I had to ask my friends to, please, keep quiet when he was there, and, although this wasn't very funny, I couldn't help laughing. He didn't believe in them, but here they were robbing him of his sleep, and he was complaining loudly about it!

Mum was very concerned about Dad; he was very poorly and she didn't think he would last much longer, so I travelled home to Fife to spend some time with them. He had deteriorated terribly, and it broke my heart to see him suffer so.

Mum had shrunk in size; she did everything for him and it was telling on her. Dad was so angry each morning to find he'd woken up, and I knew exactly how he felt. He wanted to die so badly, and even took an overdose at one point.

Mum said the doctor was so angry with her because she'd phoned for the priest instead of him.

"I reckoned his last rites were more important," was all she said.

I told him he mustn't ever try such a silly thing again. "You should know better, Dad, if you want to enter the Kingdom of Heaven," I scolded. "You've always been a good Catholic, and you have almost committed a terrible sin."

He looked sadly at me and said, "Margaret, I don't care any more." The gleam had gone from his eyes, and I knew he wouldn't be here much longer.

Before returning South, I phoned Jean, Ronnie's mother, in Edinburgh, to say I was in Fife. Although we'd kept in touch by mail, I hadn't seen Jean since I left Ronnie in 1965, and she invited me to spend my last evening in Scotland with her.

The day prior to my departure, the ambulance had

turned up to take Dad for his radium treatment. As I sat for a few minutes saying my goodbyes, I looked into his eyes. His spirit didn't dwell there any longer and my strange stomach started; I knew that my father was dying and this would be our last farewell. As he kissed me, he whispered, "See you in the next world, Margaret."

"Yes, Dad. Till then, God bless you." I watched the ambulance till it was out of sight.

During my visit, we had had a good heart-to-heart, Dad and I.

"Never walk in anyone's shadow," he'd said, "there are many paths to God, hen, and you have found yours. I just hope I've found mine."

"Oh, I'm sure you have, Dad, I'm sure you have." His doubts had begun.

Jean had phoned to say that Ronnie would come over to Fife and pick me up, to save me getting on and off trains and buses. I was pleased to see him again, and found that he was happy with his present girlfriend after his second marriage had failed. All the bitterness from the past had long gone; we were now friends, and I promised that John, who was now fifteen, could visit him for a holiday.

Jean and I chatted like there was no tomorrow. It was nice to see her, as we'd always got on well. I was sad to leave; overall, it had been quite an emotional trip.

I had phoned and asked Mick to meet me on my arrival in Margate, but he wasn't there so I hailed a taxi. Arriving home, I felt emotionally drained; the kids were out and Mick must be at work, I thought.

A neighbour's daughter called in and, as I sat talking to her, my strange stomach started. I looked at the clock; it was just before 5.15 p.m. I began to shake, and there was an urgency in me.

"I've got to phone the hospital, it's my Dad." I got straight through to Scotland and, on being connected to the ward he was in, was asked who was calling. "His daughter," I replied anxiously.

"Hold on a minute."

My heart was pounding and, as I held on, I found myself saying out loud, "Go toward the light, Dad, go toward the light."

"Hello," the nurse broke in.

"Yes," I whispered.

"I'm sorry, but your father passed away a few minutes ago."

"Thank you," I said, and gently put the phone down. It was August the 25th, 1976.

"There, there, Dad, you're all right now." His shot of radium treatment had knocked him unconscious; his body was not taking any more.

Mick seemed distant from me. At first, I thought it was because of Dad's death, so I put it out of my mind. I had to go home again to bury my father and console my mother, and Mick came with me. I was surprised to find that Auntie Anne was missing from the mourners; Uncle Matt told me she hadn't been keeping too well, so couldn't make the journey from Doncaster where they lived.

Mrs Jackson and I had a long chat; I was so pleased to see her. She had always been a good friend and always made me feel comfortable. I loved this lady very much; she was thrilled to hear of my psychic work.

"You've a long way to go yet, hen," she said, "but you'll get your message across, of that I have no doubt. You know, one of your Dad's favourite songs was 'Keep Right On To The End Of The Road'. Well, believe me, he wants you to do just that."

"Yes, I know he does, and I will," I promised her.

Mrs Jackson passed over shortly afterwards.

I went back to work, and Mrs Elias was glad to see me; within a few days, she was off on her travels again. She always seemed to go when some of the residents were dying. "You know what to do," was all she'd say before departing.

During these trips of hers, I was on call twenty-four hours a day, but I loved my work and we did have some laughs. The residents loved me being in charge, as I would give them greater portions of food than Matron ever would, and I would let them watch TV for as long as they wanted.

I was seeing less and less of Mick, but then I hadn't seen much of him for some years now. He worked every evening, now, and weekends were taken up with his banger racing. Some nights, he just didn't come home and I chose to believe his excuses.

Mum was grieving and very depressed. She missed Dad so much; after all, had he survived just another year, they would have been married for fifty years.

Brother Pat had phoned me from the States and had decided that Mum should fly over and spend some time with him and asked if I would come with her. I had told him I couldn't possibly afford it, but he told me not to worry about that. Mum, who suffered from angina, had been given the all clear by her doctor, and Mick had no objection to my going. So, Mum and I flew to California on the 21st of December 1976 and stayed for two months; I missed the kids terribly, as they had always been around me.

Pat treated us well and took us to Hollywood, all around the film stars' homes. We wandered through Lucille Ball's bungalow, and watched Robert Wagner and Eddie Albert filming their detective series.

Peter Falk was shooting a new series called 'Columbo', and we were invited to play as extras in an episode. We declined as, at that time, we didn't have it on TV here and we would have had to stay too long at the film studios. On we went to Las Vegas and Mexico, and many other interesting places.

Pat had remained a Catholic, while Frank and I had not. I was astounded at the sheer luxury of the churches and chapels there; of course, this was relatively new country, and there had been no crusaders giving churches as gifts in the U.S.A., as had been the case in Britain.

Pat had certainly moved up in life, materialistically speaking. During our stay in Las Vegas, the gambling casinos were full of celebrities and Pauline, Pat's wife, would point them out to me. At one point, Diana Ross was sitting next to me at a blackjack table; I didn't recognize her!

Farrah Fawcett-Majors looked as if she could do with a good feed. It's amazing what a bit of lipstick and paint can do; these stars were just like ordinary people that you pass every day in the street.

Mum loved playing the one armed bandits, while I enjoyed Kino, Nevada's equivalent of Bingo.

Our hotel room was luxurious; the single beds were huge and covered in leopard skin, with curtains to match. The TV showed how you could gamble, although I wasn't interested in that, while the magazines in the room offered the services of both men and women; Mum couldn't believe the catalogue of beautiful men on offer.

"Why don't you order one?" I asked her, as she flicked through the pages.

"I wouldn't know what to do with one, hen," she said. This certainly was sin city.

We brought in the New Year in Santa Monica, at a huge party for immigrants, and we all watched the count-down, coming from Times Square, on a large TV screen. It didn't mean anything to me, as my thoughts were with my kids in England. At four o'clock that New Year's Eve afternoon, I had wondered where Mick was; I was homesick.

Mum looked wonderful in a beautiful turquoise chiffon dress, but I could detect the sadness in her eyes. She was thinking of Dad. "Come on hen," she sighed, "let's get pissed."

"Good idea, Esther, good idea." So we joined in the celebrations and did just that.

Of course, never a day passed when psychic talk wouldn't be brought up. Pat wasn't sure about it, while Pauline was more interested; she took me down the street where clairvoyants dealt with clients. They charged a small fortune, too.

Pat suggested I move over to capture the American clientele; it was boom time for psychics in California. It wasn't a case of 'Who's your doctor', it was a case of 'Who's your psychic'. Neither the possible wealth, nor the suggestion, appealed to me.

However, unknown to me then, it wouldn't be long

before Americans would be travelling over to see me!

We arrived back at Heathrow where Mick was waiting for us; I was so glad to see him, and we saw Mum off on her flight to Edinburgh before we drove back to Kent. The kids were excited to see what goodies I'd brought, and they all looked well.

I'd been back at the nursing home for about eight weeks when the phone rang. It was Ronnie's mum, Jean, who told me that Ronnie was in hospital; he'd taken a severe headache a few days before and had been admitted for tests, but I was not to worry.

My strange stomach started. Oh no, I thought. I wasn't ready for this. Not Ronnie. He was due to be getting married soon. "I'll phone you back and let you know what's happening," Jean said.

I couldn't sleep. I knew what was going to happen. I deliberately wouldn't phone. I kept telling myself that Jean had said it was only a headache, so I was just getting worked up for nothing.

Two days later, Ronnie's girlfriend phoned me. Ronnie had died; he was only thirty-two and she had been so good for him. It was now April the 22nd, 1977; only eight months since my beloved father had died and a few short months after Mrs Jackson's passing. I was losing my loved ones rapidly and Mick couldn't understand why I was so upset.

There was a blazing row. Ronnie had been my first love, so of course I was upset. I wouldn't forget this scene in a hurry, either.

I phoned Mum and told her that John and I would be coming home so he could bury his father. I was so glad that John had spent some weeks with Ronnie on holiday that year.

It was such a sad occasion. He lay in his coffin and looked like an Egyptian prince; he was so handsome.

I thank God for allowing me some time with him before he died; a short time, maybe, but long enough for us to be friends once more. Sadly, his mother still grieves today, having never got over it.

I now attended the Spiritualist churches with hope in my heart that someone would send a message to me. Although I was able to give assurance and reassurance, I also needed it myself. After all, I was only human, and the gift was not for me.

Although a medium would usually pick me out, the messages I got were usually of a spiritual nature. Mrs Wedgewood was too close to me, so I needed to see someone who didn't know me.

It was suggested I go and see a Mrs McKeever, who had recently moved to the area, so Nan, another neighbour, and I went to see her. Mrs McKeever was a pleasant woman. I elected to sit first but, when I saw her produce a pack of playing cards, I felt disappointed.

She was going to tell my fortune, I thought. However, she started by saying that I should be sitting where she sat, as I was much more psychic than she could ever be. She then told me not to be put off by the cards; her spirit guide was a gypsy and the cards only acted as an aid.

She first spoke of things that I could relate to, then my father came through. I was overjoyed! He told me that the next few years would still be difficult and that I was to remain strong. Changes would have to be made and, no matter how hard it might be, I was to keep right on to the end of the road.

I was speechless! Those had been Mrs Jackson's words.

We were all thrilled with our readings and, as we drove home, I was elated. I'd finally received my message. I phoned Mum and told her, and she was thrilled.

ELEVEN

My son, John, had been attending the Spiritualist church with his friends and they'd joined a circle. He would come home singing the praises of the medium who'd sat in the circle. "Why don't you come and join it with us, Mum?" he suggested.

"No, John, I'm not interested in doing that."

He tried so hard to persuade me, but I didn't feel the need to join a circle until, one night, he told me that one of the members had left the group and, if I didn't replace her, they would have to break up. So I gave in, saying I would see what it was like, but firmly stating that I wouldn't be making a habit of it.

We arrived at the church; the medium had not yet arrived, so we sat with the others. There were about ten of them in the circle.

Suddenly, my 'voice' spoke, "You know the medium already, and will work well with her, but you work alone." I couldn't think of who it might be. Then a thought struck me; could it possibly be Mrs McKeever?

Asking John her name, he only knew her as 'Min'. I then watched a few women enter the church; Mrs McKeever was one of them. "Is that her?" I excitedly asked John.

"Yes, Mum, do you know her?"

"She's the one we went to see!"

Looking across, she came straight over to John,

who stood up and introduced me. "You're the lady I saw recently, aren't you?" she said. "Well, I'm very pleased to meet you again. John's been telling me that you do this all the time. I knew we'd see each other again and I'm thrilled that you've come to join us."

We all formed a circle. The atmosphere was lovely and I settled comfortably on a chair, not knowing what to expect. I looked around at everyone else. All eyes were closed, so I followed suit. This was new to me.

Mrs McKeever said a prayer, then we all sat quietly. You could have heard a pin drop. As I sat, completely relaxed, my strange stomach started and I fidgeted slightly. My 'voice' told me not to worry, so I relaxed again. A force of energy was moving through my solar plexus and up towards my throat, which I felt the need to clear.

Although my eyes were closed, I could see Mrs McKeever watching me. A guttural sound was coming from my being. I watched Mrs McKeever move closer. No one else moved. All were sat with eyes firmly closed. Quietly, she spoke, "Welcome friend, please speak with us." With that, a man's voice boomed out of my throat.

I couldn't move. I had been taken over, yet I could see everyone in the circle and I felt terrific. My spirit was slightly to the side of my body, not in it. By now, I noticed, everyone had opened their eyes and were looking toward me.

The man said, "Beatty, darling," and Beatty, one of the sitters, answered. The visitor was her late husband. My hands began to move while the man spoke; Beatty explained, later, that her husband had used those same mannerisms when he was here on earth. His features were also seen clearly on my face; this, I was told, was known as 'transfiguration'.

It was a very emotional reunion between Beatty and her husband: marvellous, to say the least. Excitement filled the church. Mrs McKeever thanked Beatty's husband and asked him to, please, leave the medium now. I felt a 'hoosh' and our friend was gone. I was back in my body.

There was a queue of spirit visitors wanting to communicate. Mrs McKeever suggested that only one more should talk; she didn't want me to tire out.

The next visitor was not recognized by anyone; he had been a schoolmaster in Wales and he was very upset at how he'd treated the pupils in his care. "Barbaric," he explained. Tears were streaming down my face, yet they were not mine.

He said he had pounded religion into his boys in a fearful way and, when he arrived on the spirit side, he had realised that he had wasted a great part of his life dominating his charges. His teachings had been wrong and he was full of remorse.

"I have to set the record straight," he went on. "There is no one here waiting to punish; I saw my life unfold before me and I'm ashamed of what I did. I must pay my retribution. I was so afraid to die, yet all I found here was love." By the time he left, he felt much better, as he'd been able to bare his soul.

"Go in peace, dear friend," Mrs McKeever said, "and God Bless You."

Once more, I moved back into my body. "We have finished for now, Margaret, how do you feel?" My eyes opened; I felt on top of the world. Both worlds, in fact. Mrs McKeever closed the circle with a prayer, and the excitement was tremendous. My only disappointment was that, although I had heard everything, I had been unable to see the spirit visitors from where my spirit had been, just beside my body. No matter. This had been a beautiful experience.

We all moved to the coffee bar and, by the time we left, it was the middle of the night. There had been so much to discuss; Mrs McKeever was a mountain of knowledge.

Min McKeever was so pleased when I related the happenings to her. "You're on your way now, Margaret," she said. "You are a true channel for spirit."

I couldn't wait for the following week when we would meet again. It was explained to me that I was a natural medium and society had not suppressed my psychic gifts.

"You have no fear in you, love," Millie said, "because you have been familiar with the spirit side all your life and you know they would never harm you."

Yes, I knew that was true.

"Perhaps, also, you now understand why life has not been too kind to you."

"Oh, it hasn't been so bad," I said.

Millie told me that she would continue to develop my mediumship until further instructions from the spirit side. After that first evening, my chair was placed in the middle of the circle; my hair was swept from my face, and a dark cover was placed around my neck and shoulders, in order to provide a clear view of spirit visitors.

This, as I have already mentioned, is known as

transfiguration, and we were never disappointed. Within a few minutes of my sitting in the chair, my strange stomach would start and spirit visitors would start arriving.

There was Mary, who had passed on the eve of her wedding and had been buried in her wedding dress. She communicated with her sister.

There was George, returning to his wife after being tragically killed in a car accident. Even dogs, cats and birds filled the room, all returning to their owners. Philosophers spoke of life on the spirit side and eagerly answered any questions. Spiritual enlightenment was taking place, in our little church, in the middle of Margate.

Our altar was a solid oak table and, one night, it was decided that we should move it by levitation. We all gathered round and lightly placed our fingertips on top of it. It lifted almost to the ceiling. We also succeeded in levitating a smaller table, which floated the length of the church before settling down at the other end.

We were visited by clowns and a weight-lifter, all of whom had been with a circus owned by a family known as the Sangers.

I had never had occasion to visit Margate Cemetery but, one evening, one of our communicators was Mr Sanger himself. He told us there was a life-size horse on his tomb; some knew of it, so John and I headed there early the following morning to view this marvel. It was wonderful standing there, looking at the horse, knowing that, only a few hours before, we had had a conversation with the very gentleman buried underneath.

Arriving home from the nursing home one afternoon, I found a group of eight ladies sitting on the garden wall. They were all from London and staying at a convalescent home nearby, and they had heard about me from a few of their friends to whom I had given readings while they had been at the same home. They were a happy lot, all Cockneys, and I invited them in and saw each one.

Never have I questioned a sitter during a reading. I have only ever asked their name so that I can relate to them, and insist that they say only 'yes' or 'no'. If there is a problem, then my guide talks about it; this is amazing in itself, as he does tend to go into some detail.

I never, ever, guarantee any communicators from the spirit side, and always explain that I can't bring the dead back. They come through themselves. If I don't hear or see anyone, I can't relate anything.

Within this group of Cockney ladies, Rose was the comical one who kept us all laughing.

During her reading, it came to light that her elderly mother had already lived with her for some years, and my guide told her that her mother would be here for a few years yet. Rose immediately put her hands on her head and said, "Oh no! I'm sick to death of her - she's become a pain in the arse. Please ask your guide if he could take her before then; she'd much rather be on the spirit side, anyway, because my dad is there."

We fell about laughing. Here was I, thinking she was being given comfort, when this particular news was bad news as far as she was concerned.

Exactly two years later, Rose informed me that her mother had passed, just as my guide had forecast.

Before they left, they asked what my charge was. I said I didn't charge anything.

"But you must charge something!"

I refused, but said, "If you feel like giving me something, you can buy me a packet of cigarettes."

Next morning, two hundred cigarettes were deposited on my doorstep, with a note saying, 'See you next year, love,' signed by the whole group.

It was at this time that I decided to contact a brother of my mother, as letters to the Salvation Army and Police Departments in various Australian states hadn't brought any luck, so I telephoned the Hertfordshire number given to me in 1973.

How was I going to explain myself? I was going to come straight out with it. This was the only way; I'd been told that already. "May I speak to Mr MacDonald, please?" I asked the lady who answered the telephone. She called him.

"Hello," I said hurriedly. "You don't know me, but I am your sister Mary's daughter, and I was wondering if I could come and see you?"

There was a pregnant pause, after which he said, "Where do you live?"

"In Kent," I answered, my heart by this time pounding.

"Can you come up on Saturday?"

"Yes, of course."

Confirming his address, he said goodbye.

I put the phone down. Well, that was straight to the point. I had to sit down for a few minutes. I was, at last, going to meet a blood relative. I gave myself a good talking to. "Take it as it comes. Remember what Millie said: don't expect too much."

Mick didn't think it was such a good idea, but I was quite determined. I couldn't believe how calm I was as we drove up to Hertfordshire and pulled up outside the house.

Aunt Molly answered the door, and I found myself standing in front of Uncle Hugh.

Cordially, we shook hands, and he asked to speak to me privately. We went into the dining-room; I sat at one end of the red velvet-covered dining table and he at the other. He questioned me closely. While I was telling him all I knew, he looked at me, his eyes misted, and he began to cry. He was my mother's elder brother and had known of my existence; he was the only member of the family who had. My mother had been over on holiday in England only two years earlier, and I'd missed her. I could have kicked myself! Had I followed up my enquiries back in 1973, I might have already met her.

People began to arrive at the house, all relatives. Uncle Jimmy was my mother's younger brother; I liked him straight away. Jackie was his wife, and I liked her too. There seemed to be a never-ending stream of nieces and nephews, all shaking hands with me. It was overwhelming.

Photographs of my mother were brought out. Aunt Molly had told me she had watched from the window as I had got out of the car and was amazed at the resemblance between my mother and myself. It was an emotional day and, at the end of it, it was difficult to remain composed while one of the family played 'Welcome Home' by Peters and Lee.

Driving back to Kent, my mother's address safely tucked away in my bag, I reflected on all the years I had dreamed of finding someone who really belonged to me.

That day, my dream had become a reality. I felt too excited to go to sleep, and penned a long letter to my mother in Australia. I felt that the sooner I sent it, the sooner I would hear from her.

All I had really found out was that she had married for the first time at the age of forty; her husband, an Australian, had been twenty-four and an entertainer. They had gone to live in Australia after their marriage in 1957, which was just after I had left Dunoon.

I also wrote a lengthy letter to Esther, telling her all about the wonderful event. In her reply, although pleased for me, she said that she still felt that I shouldn't get too carried away. She was obviously very depressed, and I suggested that she should come down and live with me, but she declined, saying that she'd spent all her life in Fife and, when her time came, she wanted to be buried with Dad and James. That was all she had to look forward to.

Our weekly meetings at church continued, and more and more people came seeking comfort and asking for guidance. My student days were over; I was now teaching as well.

Bill was a gentleman who had been involved in Spiritualism for many years and, while I was in trance one evening, our visitor began to speak to him.

"Hiya, buddy," he said.

Bill answered, "Hello, who are you, friend?"

"You know who I am!"

"No, I don't," said Bill. "What's your name?"

"You know my name, buddy."

A conversation began between the two, yet the

spirit visitor would not give Bill his name. I was puzzled; I couldn't understand why Bill was so insistent. The guy told Bill of how he'd been shot by the Nazis, and answered all the questions put to him. Yet, throughout his visit, he would not divulge his name.

I soon found out why. When our seance had finished, Bill came over, put his arms around me, and told me that his visitor had been his brother. For years, Bill had visited mediums and attended seances in the hope of some communication from him. The fact that the visitor would only call him 'buddy' was the evidence that Bill needed; they had only ever referred to each other by that name.

Bill had at last found a communication from his 'buddy' that he could accept. He was full of hope; his brother had given him details of where his remains could be found, and Bill had every intention of following up the lead.

"Oh, Bill, wouldn't it be marvellous if you could find him after all these years?" I said.

"Yes, it's my life's dream and, this time, I feel certain I will find him. Bill went home that night from church an elated soul; we would all follow this spirit message with great interest."

Millie and I had discussed the possibility of hiring a hall and inviting people to come for discussion and communication, on which she and I would work together. We secured a church hall for two pounds a week, commenced a few weeks afterwards, and were very pleased with the results - until my guide told me that I must give the keys back.

We did as we were told, finding out from the caretaker that the vicar was going mad, as someone had told him that seances were being held in his church hall. That ended our weekly meetings. However, the word had got around, so both Millie's and my home were always full of people, asking questions and gaining enlightenment on life after death.

Life holds many mysteries. We can't understand many of them, but I would like to tell you about one.

Mavis, a reflexologist and member of the developing group at church, had invited me for tea one afternoon at her rambling old house. We spent a pleasant afternoon in her music room and, before I left, Mavis invited me to return the following week.

On being shown, once more, into the music room, I was surprised to see the difference in the decor after only one week. When I commented on the changes, Mavis looked at me and told me that the room was exactly the same as it had been before. However, I was able to describe the couch I had sat on, the carpet, and even the fireplace, all of which had now changed.

Quite calmly, Mavis left the room, to return with a faded, gold-coloured cushion, that had once been part of the couch I had sat on the previous week. She told me that I had described the room as it had been in the fifties, prior to her husband's death. This was amazing, to say the least.

"What had happened to me?" I asked.

"You experienced a time lapse. Some people have found themselves in another time without realising it, with everything as it had been, with people from that era the same as they were then, going about their daily life."

This revelation completely puzzled me; I just

couldn't understand it. It certainly was a mystery, so I asked my guide to explain. This is what he said:

"If you take a picture with a camera, you have captured that event forever. Yourself as a child, perhaps. Years later, on your plane of existence, you can look back and nothing on that photograph will have changed, but you will have. Every event in your world is captured. Time is eternal. Therefore, anything that has taken place, cannot be changed."

"But why did I find myself in that situation from the fifties here in Kent, when I was actually in Scotland during those years?"

"The eye is also a camera, forever focusing, taking in all in its scope. From there, it is forever computerised into the mind."

"But isn't it true that the eye can sometimes play tricks on you?"

"Yes," he said, "but that is the mind working ahead of the camera and, in that sense, full concentration is not being used. Therefore, the picture becomes distorted, as can a photograph, if the user of the camera hasn't set the sight straight and concentrated properly."

"Heavy stuff, this," I laughed.

"No, it is very understandable," he replied.

I had been given my explanation and accepted it without further question; after all, he was the boss.

TWELVE

A letter with AIR MAIL and from Australia! This was the moment I'd been waiting for; it was from my mother. At six weeks since I sent my letter, I had begun to think I would never hear from her.

She told me she had been shocked to read my letter, as she had thought that I had died; the Welfare had told her this and, after her mother had been murdered, she had left the area. She never explained what I was doing living with a friend in the first place.

She went on to tell me about my father; how she felt she didn't love him enough to marry him. Uncle Hugh, she confirmed, was the only person to know about my birth. She said she had a confession to make, and wanted to tell it now.

While married to her young husband, life had become unbearable; she had killed him and had served fifteen years' imprisonment in Australia for her crime. I have never tried to find out the exact circumstances. She asked my forgiveness, and said she would understand if I did not want to write to her any more. She told me how she had desperately wanted another child, but I had been the only one.

Not knowing what to think, I showed Millie the letter and asked her advice. Millie said it was not for me to judge, telling me that my mother's debt to society had been paid and, although there was never any excuse for the taking of a human life, perhaps this was the reason why I had to find her. God works in mysterious ways, she added. Psychometrising the letter, Millie felt that a very lonely, very unhappy, human being was calling out, and suggested I should answer the letter. I did, and, in doing so, gave this lady, who brought me into this world, a new lease of life.

I had phoned my mother's younger brother, Uncle Jimmy, and the rest of the family, inviting them to come down for the weekend; we all got on tremendously well. During that visit we went out for the evening and, on our return, were chatting about psychic things when Jimmy, five parts to the wind, confessed that he'd also been hearing voices since he was a child, but had ignored them.

Jackie confirmed that he, too, would hold conversations with the spirit side while asleep.

Jimmy was sceptical, and said so.

"How can you be sceptical about something you know nothing about?", I asked.

"What is there to know?"

"There's the knowledge that we cannot die, and proof of it. Our spirits are eternal – our schooling has taught us this – but we tend to disregard the fact when it happens."

"Yes," said Jimmy, "but no one knows for sure."

"The difference between people like us and the clergy," I answered, "is that we can prove it and bring comfort. Cold comfort isn't given by us. Death frightens people and that is very sad."

"Well, I don't know," Jimmy said, "I think we should leave well alone," and off he went to bed.

Jackie was amazed. "Do you know, that's the first time he has ever admitted to anyone about hearing his voices. He used to tell me I was talking rubbish when I mentioned his conversations."

My nephew, Clive, decided he was going to develop his abilities and, although Jackie said she would support him, she would leave it alone herself. Today, Jackie is still sitting in a development circle and has taken more of an interest than Clive!

At church one evening, I was most delighted when Mrs McKeever's late husband and grandson came through. She told me afterwards that she had hoped that they might, as that particular day was the anniversary of the day they had drowned together while fishing.

Another visitor arrived that night, a very unhappy soul, lost and needing to be rescued. I will have to call him Joe Bloggs. He cried and cried for his wife and son, and didn't know where to find them. He had committed a terrible deed, he said, and needed forgiveness from them.

During this time, I had also been doing automatic writing. It had taken many months of holding pen and paper without any results until, one evening, the pen began to flow and spirit writing began to appear.

Not long after the visit of Joe Bloggs, I was sitting at home and had a great urge to pick up my pen; this lost soul gave information which included the address of his wife.

With the aid of a friend, who works for the DHSS in the Midlands area, I checked out the address. It had, in fact, been there until a few months before, when the whole street had been demolished; Joe Bloggs had been an earthbound spirit and, when his home had gone, he had found himself lost and distressed.

Being in trance during his visit at church, I had been unable to see him. I now asked him to show himself, which he did; he gave me a telephone number, and I wrote it down. It was quite a shock, on getting through, to find it was the number of a prison Governor's hot line and only available through the Home Office! How was I going to explain this?

Joe Bloggs had told me he was a prisoner killed in a prison riot; the prison also has to remain nameless. Joe Bloggs arrived safely on the spirit side, sure of the forgiveness of his beloved family, and I managed to keep out of trouble with the authorities by destroying everything I had written.

It was now nearing the end of September 1978. I woke up one night to find Esther, my mother, sitting on my bed. I looked at the luminous dial on the clock; it read 3.15 a.m. I woke Mick up to tell him that my mum had died. He told me to get back to sleep. My strange stomach was on me; I knew Esther had passed over.

On looking out of my top stair window just after nine that morning, I knew that the telegram man, heading down the street, was delivering to me. I met him at the door. Opening the telegram, I read:

MUM FOUND DEAD FRANK STOP

It was the 29th of September. Esther had let me know that she had passed over, and I would be making my last journey to Fife to bury my mother beside her beloved husband and son. I was so very sad; we had only just got to know each other, and I loved this lady so much. Once again, I felt so alone.

Mum's family doctor said that she had died suddenly between 12.15 am and 7.30 am. Her cousin had left her at around midnight, when Mum, in good spirits, had begun to prepare for bed.

The neighbour who had found her at 8 am told me that Mum had been sitting up on the bed, back against the wall, facing the pillow; in fact, just as I had seen her at 3.15. When I described the cotton nightie I had seen her wearing, Mum's neighbour looked at me strangely and asked how I could possibly know that she'd been wearing that particular one.

I explained, and she told me how Mum had always talked about my gift and had, only earlier that day, told her she had decided that she would move down beside me.

Just as at Dad's funeral, Auntie Anne was once more missing from the mourners. Uncle Matt sat me down and told me Auntie Anne had severed ties between herself and Mum some years before, when she realized the cruelty that had been administered to me.

The last straw, he said, came when they had all visited me in Edinburgh, when I was married to Ronnie, and Mum had slapped me hard around the face for forgetting to salt the potatoes. I had embarrassed her in front of Auntie Anne. This explanation left me feeling very bad.

"Well, it was stupid of me; I should not have forgotten to salt them!"

"But you were nervous, you were also a married woman, and Esther had no right to hit you for it."

I could not defend my mother in this instance; Uncle Matt felt the same as Auntie Anne, and we all went our separate ways.

Back home, I could not settle; I just could not understand how calmly I had dealt with Mum's funeral. I continued to work, dealing with old people, ill and dying.

My marriage, I felt, was now a sham, and Mick still could not accept my psychic work.

"Don't you think it's time you gave up all this psychic nonsense?" he put to me during an argument.

"Don't you think you should give up drinking and women?" I snapped back. "If you're giving me an ultimatum, then you lose, Mick. I've got you in this lifetime, but I've got God and his work forever." I then told him our marriage was over.

I woke up one morning at the end of October 1978 and I knew that, if Mick and I remained together, we would be prolonging an agony for both of us and the kids. We had been married for ten years and seven months. Although I did not realize it then, I was in deep distress; no one knew about it, especially myself.

Having been told that a new medium would be giving clairvoyance the following Monday afternoon, I took my seat in the packed church.

The President began to speak of this gifted person, and hoped we would all send our loving thoughts to her on this, her first public demonstration. Then, suddenly, my name was called out and I was asked to take the platform.

I was shocked, but felt I couldn't refuse in front of so many people. So, I gave out the messages that afternoon. Those attending were thrilled at my deliverance and congratulated me afterwards, but I was angry and upset at having been tricked into it. I had been told many times that I was to work alone, and was to remain unbiased as far as any religion was concerned.

That was when I chose to call myself a Spiritist. I do, however, respect anyone's need for a religion; for many it is important, for me it is not. Eternal life is for all; my guide, in his teachings, didn't feel it was necessary for me to mention it. After all, we were all to be under the same roof at the end of the day.

From that afternoon, I refused to do any more public work; I would not go against my guide's instructions.

One evening, Mrs McKeever took me aside and told me that she had taken me as far as she could and that I was to find an advanced medium. She also asked me if I had been developing with another couple, as talk of this had been going around members of the church.

I assured her that I had not been developing anywhere else, only with her. I admired and respected this medium so much, I would not even consider sitting anywhere else. "That's good enough for me," she said, "but you must understand that there is as much jealousy and bitchiness in this religion as there is in others. I believe what you tell me, but I can't take you any further; my limits will not allow."

Where was I going to find an advanced medium? I advertised in the Psychic News and, after about six weeks wait, received a reply. Adam announced he would sit with me every Monday.

We had arranged to hold our weekly meetings at Mavis' house, as interruptions would be few; there were no children there. Adam, a gentleman in his sixties, told us he had never had any dealings with spirit side until, one day, after being given only a few weeks to live, he'd heard a voice speak to him. He immediately thought he was on his way out.

Again, the voice spoke, suggesting to him that, if he chose to work for spirit, his health would return.

Laughingly, he told the voice that, if they could return his health, he would certainly work for them. Within the three weeks he had left, Adam was back to health, his doctor saying that a wrong diagnosis must have been made. Since then, he had been visiting circles and receiving instruction from spirit side. I remember seeing his guide, a tall, tall, man who reminded me of one of the natives I had once seen in the film, 'King Solomon's Mines'. A long neck, covered in gold necklets. When I described what I had seen, Adam confirmed that this native was his guide, who gave him instructions for him to carry out.

(I would like, at this point to quash the Victorian idea that seances must be held in a darkened room, with a red light. As electric light can endanger the medium, these conditions are, however, necessary for certain aspects of communication and are used mainly for the protection of the medium.)

We sat without drawn curtains or red lights, achieving communication just the same.

I viewed the gentleman before me. He was wearing a dirty-looking kilt, had a shock of red hair round his face and his head, and held a bottle of Scotch, which I watched him swig from. His name was John Brown, he said, Gillie to Queen Victoria, and did he swear! The air was blue.

Then, I found myself looking toward a young lady who was holding her knee. She had hurt it and was relating how she had fallen over and scraped it.

From photographs I had seen, I was able to establish that she was the future Queen Mary. I hadn't been aware that John Brown had had red hair, and this fact amused me very much.

My mother, Esther, was another arrival. I was filled with her emotions as she told me she couldn't find Dad. Esther needed rescuing and I was able to help her, with a great deal of love, to reach the spirit side.

I sat with Adam for only about a month, as I didn't feel that I was doing any more than I had in church. The only significant difference was the daylight.

Continuing my healing and readings, I found more and more people able, at last, to 'talk to someone who could understand' about thoughts and feelings they felt unable to express as freely as they would like.

After a visit from a lovely lady who had lost her son, ill for three years prior to his passing, I found her vicar on my doorstep. I invited him in, and he sat down and began to tell me he didn't feel I was doing her any good by 'filling her head with such nonsense'.

"But surely, this is what your church is all about," I countered, "that life is eternal." I quickly added, "At least she left here happier than when she left your church. After her visit here, she's confident that her son lives on."

Ignoring my reply, he went on to ask me how much money I was making out of the grief of others and telling me how wrong I was.

I told him I didn't make any money, as I never took a penny from anybody for my work, and how could he be so bold as to accuse me, when he lived in a fine house, had a nice car, housekeeper, and all his bills paid at the expense of his parishioners, while I was struggling to bring up three kids on next to nothing.

Well, he didn't like that one bit.

"You prove to me there is life after death," he said, "and I'll come and work with you," to which I replied, "You prove to me there isn't, and I'll come and work with you."

He muttered on about my being in league with the Devil, and we bid each other good-day.

That evening, I had a call to go and give some healing to a lady who was dying. The journey would take me to Canterbury; it was nine o'clock at night and, as I set out, the snow was falling heavily.

Now, some people may say, 'Why bother to go that far when a lady's death is imminent?' To which I would say, 'We don't know if any healing will work, we are only channels; but, if it doesn't, then the comfort given is sufficient.' As it was on this particular occasion, and on many since.

The lady passed while I held her hand and prayed. Leaving for my journey home, I was weary and sad. The heater on the car wasn't working and I didn't know if I'd have enough petrol to get me home. It was still snowing, 1.30 in the morning, and my petrol gauge told me I was not going to make it.

About two miles from home, the car gave up and I walked the rest of the way, arriving home feeling totally exhausted. I was suffering from delayed grief; I didn't realize it, but it was on me now.

I was still taking pills given to me by my doctor some years before, and now he handed me some more. I was hazy for the next few months. Nan, my neighbour, was beside me for hours on end every day, soothing me.

All the years of cruelty, humiliation, disloyalty,

separation, and all I felt was my fault, had taken their toll. I screamed at Mum for leaving me, and at Ronnie for all the wrong I thought he'd done, asking him to help me now.

"What happened to your bloody wedding ring? I always wore it, where is it now when I need comfort?" I cried. "It was the only thing I had at the end of our marriage." Twisting Mum's wedding ring round my finger, I was on the verge of a nervous breakdown and, no matter how positive I tried to be, this thing had me beaten.

I would come to, sitting on the seashore and not knowing how I got there. I would walk out in front of traffic without seeing it. I didn't know what day of the week it was.

I can understand how poor souls commit suicide; they are sick and don't know what is going on. I believe that no amount of pills will cure anyone but, instead, completely control their lives and keep reality from them; for emotional problems, pills in the long term are not a remedy, but a suppressant.

My turning point came one morning when I phoned my doctor and told him I had to be taken away; I couldn't cope with anything any more. I didn't know what I was doing, and told him how, only half an hour before, I'd been seeing the kids off to school, and fifteen minutes later I'd been pacing the street, telling a neighbour they were late home from school and something must have happened to them.

My doctor told me to go and pack a few things in a suitcase; he would phone Mick to collect the kids and would send a car for me.

The man in the car was a voluntary worker who

was to take me to a hospital where, my doctor reckoned, a few days rest would do me good.

On arrival at the hospital, I was given a cup of tea by a cheery-looking nurse. I couldn't even hold the cup, I was shaking so much.

The following morning I saw a doctor, the hospital psychiatrist and, after chatting to me, he told me I was suffering from deep stress, brought on by grief. There was nothing they could do for me but, although he felt it was up to me to pull myself together, I was welcome to stay a few days at least.

I believe this was the jolt I needed. I walked into the empty day-room, looking out of the window at the trees swaying gently, and watching a squirrel run across the lawn. I just broke down and cried and cried. The last time I recall crying so much was when I was first taken back to Glasgow all those years ago.

The next day, I was ready to go home and my recovery began. I owe so much to Nan for her patience with me during this, a very difficult period in my life.

I threw myself back into my work and, on Millie's advice, began charging one pound for a sitting. "After all," Millie had said, "you are providing a service and you, too, have bills to pay; let's face it, if people are willing to give something, they feel they can come back."

I'd never thought of it like that before, but she was right. So, from now on, readings would cost one pound, but both healing and teaching would be free.

Mrs Elias had sold the nursing home, having left me to deal with prospective buyers while she was on one of her jaunts abroad, but one of my sitters worked for the Social Services Department; their head man came to see me and offered me a job with them, and I gladly took it. However, I couldn't handle this work for too long, as I felt that these people who, like the clergy, worked from theory, didn't have any practical experience of problems in family life, so therefore didn't show much compassion where it was most needed, with the children. However, I was well educated in psychology and was offered a place at the Open University. It was now 1981, and I felt better than I had for many years.

My dear friend, Millie, had passed over to the spirit side; she had achieved her purpose in this life and had gone on to collect her rewards.

I now felt it was time for clearing up in my life, so I decided the time was right for my divorce from Mick; we were friends and still continued to be so.

I continued to write to my real mother in Australia, but with no great yearn to see her. I also decided to move house. Penny had said she was going to have a holiday abroad and invited me to accompany her at her expense, saying I could do with the break.

Mick took the children away for a fortnight's holiday while Penny and I went off to Morocco. North Africa was a beautiful place, and I fell in love with it the minute I stepped off the plane.

Our hotel was grand, and situated on the main seafront, offering us a magnificent view of the sea and the ships. The sands were pure white. It was exquisite.

The line of the Marrakesh Express lay in front of us, such an insignificant-looking line to be afforded such grandeur in the song made famous by Simon and Garfunkel.

As we journeyed by taxi to the kasbah one morning, our taxi driver stopped to pick up another fare on the way, as was the custom.

On entering the car, the passenger spoke to the driver in Arabic and I realised that I knew what he was saying. I was shocked, but turned to Penny and repeated what he had said.

"Ask him, ask him," she said excitedly.

"Did he just give you an address on so-and-so street to take him to?" I asked the driver.

The driver smiled at me and said, "Ah, you understand Arabic."

But I didn't. I couldn't speak a word of the language. Another lesson was being given to me: that language is not a barrier between worlds.

I was amazed, then, to see before me, as large as life, my Chinese guide. My main man. Dressed in purple and gold, his pigtail hanging way down his back.

"What's your name?" I whispered.

"My name is Chang Li," he answered. I was beside myself with joy. It had taken him almost forty years to introduce himself to me and, of all places, he chose to do so in Africa.

We had been there for a week when, while having lunch in a restaurant, I could feel I was being watched. Turning round, I saw an old Arab gentleman staring at me. Seeing me look towards him, he approached and began to speak to me in Arabic, which I could not understand. So I called the waiter over to interpret, to be told the old Arab was telling me I was the reincarnation of Nefertiti. I shuddered at this revelation from a stranger, as he wasn't to know my feelings about Egypt, nor the emotions that overcame me whenever I saw or read about that land.

Our interpreter told us this man was a Shaman, and Penny promptly told him of my work in England. That was it. I spent most of the time we had left giving readings to Arabs but, of course, through an interpreter.

The most uncanny things were given and accepted. The Arab who was told by my guide that he would soon have the boy he wished for; we found that this man's wife was, at that moment, about to give birth, and delivered her baby the same evening. It was the boy he had hoped for.

The gentleman who would have to have an operation on his eye, who confirmed he was going into hospital the following week to have it done. Any problems in his eye were not apparent by merely looking at him.

Many, many recipients were thrilled to bits by their readings. Our stay went much too quickly and we left, having made good friends of these lovely people and other fellow holiday makers.

On my return, Mick helped me move house; to a happy house, in which I still live. It has a beautiful atmosphere, a fact which has not gone unmentioned by many of the people who have crossed its threshold.

I hold a grand collection of brass, mostly Egyptian, a passion I have had for many years. Unknown to me when the Arab Shaman told me of my reincarnation, but a fact made known to me since, brass was used in Egypt by seers and prophets to ward off evil spirits.

Had I unknowingly been protecting myself all these

years? Had I been here before? Was this my reason for crying over Egypt? Perhaps. But the bond is there and will not be broken. I know one thing for sure, as do my family and close friends, that each time I decide to go to Egypt, I begin to shiver and won't go.

I did, however, go back to Morocco, this time through the generosity of an old Polish gentleman who had been amazed when his sister communicated with him from the spirit side. She, together with her two sons, had been killed by German soldiers during the war, when she had tried to defend her home. When he passed, this kind gentleman left me two thousand pounds as a thank you. This also enabled me to return the favour to Penny; this time, we visited Agadir, a few hundred miles further into Africa.

THIRTEEN

It was April 1983 and, answering the doorbell one morning at 8.30 am, I was surprised to see Mick standing there. Asking what was wrong, he replied, "Nothing, but I brought this over. Mum found it and thought it must be yours."

On opening the envelope he handed me, I took out Ronnie's wedding ring. I was overwhelmed.

"But how could she have found it, Mick? We searched everywhere for it!"

"She just found it in a drawer."

Ronnie, I believe, had returned my ring. He had, indeed, heard my cry in the wilderness when I most needed it to be heard. The date was April the 22nd, six years to the day since he had passed, and fifteen years since the ring had gone missing. I'd finally got it back, it still fitted, and I still wear it today, together with my mother's ring.

Janet, a nurse at the hospital, arrived with a group of friends. Saying that she was just with them but felt no need for a reading, she sat in the garden; however, before long, her friends coaxed her into seeing me.

During her reading, my guide suggested healing on a back complaint that had dogged her for many years. She admitted to wearing a surgical corset, and allowed me to give her healing; after this, she removed the corset and has never worn it since. She's still nursing and has had no further problems with her back. Janet had been a non-believer.

I was now receiving requests for postal readings from the United States, Canada, North Africa and Paris, as well as the U.K. There were not enough hours in the day for me, especially since I had started work in another nursing home, as a care assistant on night duty, where I would work from 8 pm to 8 am.

I had taken in a few students who were visiting this country in order to learn English. I would go to bed around 9 am each morning, and a friend of mine would come in at midday and wake me up with a cuppa. After this, I would do my readings or go and have a game of bingo with her for a few hours, feed the kids and our students, then go back on duty at eight o'clock. This was for four nights a week.

I loved my job very much. My old people were terrific; before I gave them breakfast each morning, although some were rickety, I would have them all standing in front of the TV doing exercises with Lizzie Webb. I felt it was good for them; every morning, I would find them all standing in front of the TV, waiting for me to switch it on!

Annie was the Matron of the nursing home and this is her addition to the book:

"I just met Mags (Margaret), as she will always be to me, when I was Matron of the nursing home; I interviewed her for the job of a night care assistant. There was I, a dyed-in-the-wool sceptic as far as the spirit world goes, finding myself so drawn to this lady with the beautiful blue eyes.

We used to cross paths in the morning, as I was coming on duty and she was going off. I found myself getting there earlier so we could have a chat. Me firing questions, her giving answers with never a falter. Eventually, of course, I was curious enough to have a reading.

All I can tell you is that I cried buckets when my mother, who had died in 1975, came through and told me what a mess my life was in; of course I knew how I felt, but no one else did.

Even after all this, I still had to question, and the crunch came when I asked why my mum didn't use my nickname any more; she always had when she was this side. I had left a note to this effect for Mags one night and, arriving on duty in the morning, had an answer from her. In the form of a riddle, she wrote the words 'HELLO TO PUT BACKWARDS'.

I puzzled over this for quite a while, then it hit me like a thunderclap. My nickname was 'Tup' which, of course, is 'Put,' backwards. I questioned no more but, as if Mum was really trying to make me even more sure, she took Mags round the house where I was born and brought up. Correct in every exact detail.

Since this time, I have had numerous things happen, too many for space to allow me to write all. But, one day, it culminated in me getting poems from the spirit side. There was I writing poetry, when I have never in my life been able to do this. It happened over a period of about six weeks and then, as quickly as it started, it stopped and I haven't done any since.

So, here you have a hardened sceptic in '83, to someone who wrote poems for spirit side in '88, firmly believing that there is a spirit world and that they will contact us, but only through love, which is such a wonderful thing. I am so very glad that they sent Mags to me.

Ann Hewitt"

A selection of Annie's poems from the spirit side will be found at the back of this book.

George Watson rang: could I see his wife? She needed healing. Asking him not to tell me her problem, I gave him an appointment to bring her along. I sat her down and proceeded, my guide telling me she was grieving and confused.

Her husband was surprised at my ability to diagnose her condition. It seems her mother had passed two years before; they had been very close and the daughter would not accept her mother's passing.

Although his wife had been under a psychiatrist for over a year, George hadn't seen any improvement; in fact, he felt she was getting worse. He'd given up a good job with an airline to look after her full-time, doing everything while she sat knitting, unwinding the result, and knitting it up again.

I saw George's wife every week for three months. She recovered.

One of the most heart-rending cases dealt with was Mandy's. After a desperate plea from her grandmother, late one night in 1984, I drove up to the house.

Mandy, a twin, was nine years old and had had a stroke which had left her blind and paralysed. I was wary, as Ruby, her grandmother, had told me that Mandy's parents did not believe. Mandy had been in the Great Ormond Street Hospital for six weeks and had just been released; nothing else could be done.

I found her curled up on the couch, with a blanket over her; all alone in her world of darkness in which, just six weeks ago, there had been light. Her twin sister watching from another chair, I sat down on the couch and drew her up to me.

She was terrified. Her parents watched helplessly, and I could immediately sense hostility from her mother.

"What are you going to do?" she demanded.

"I'm just going to hold her for a minute, and then put my hands on her head," I answered.

I prayed so hard to myself and don't know how I didn't break down. She was so thin and helpless. I should explain, at this point, that, when healing anyone, I take the condition onto myself, feeling every ache and pain in the same area as the recipient.

As healing began, I could see out of one eye; a misty view, just a silhouette. The heat going through Mandy was terrific; water was dripping from my hands and trickling down my face and back.

When I had finished, Mandy would not let me go, clung very tight and, thinking I was going to let her go, just said, "Margaret!" and held on tighter. I soothed her and made a bold statement.

I told her parents she would be able to walk within a few days and, although I could not see out of one eye, there definitely was vision in the other. Her mother then told me that the doctors at Great Ormond Street had said that one eye had been completely destroyed when she had had the stroke. An appointment for physiotherapy had been made at our local general hospital, to try and strengthen her withering legs; they had been marvellous with Mandy, but had done all they could.

"I don't doubt that," I replied, "but we will have to wait and see if any improvement will take place." I then asked if I could call back again, and was given permission, since Mandy had obviously taken to me so much.

I didn't have to wait long for my next visit. Three days later Mandy's mother rang me, "Can you come up?" she asked. "What's wrong, love?" I asked, hesitantly.

"Mandy's walking," she declared.

"Thank the Lord!" I shouted, and was up to see her as soon as I could. There she was, standing by herself, her father talking her towards him. Precariously moving one foot in front of the other, she fell into her father's arms. The house was full of relatives and we all laughed and cried at the same time. Ruby, her grandmother, gave me a big cuddle, all the payment I would need. Her mother joyfully said, "Wait till they see her walk in for her physiotherapy treatment, are they in for a surprise!"

Not long after, Mandy regained her sight, in the eye I had been able to see through myself.

On relating the events to Annie, she took it matter-of-factly, saying, "Well, darling, you have a beautiful gift and you use it wisely."

"Yes," I replied, "I have the gift, and I thank God for bestowing it on me."

I next sat with a lady doctor, from Great Ormond Street; she'd travelled far, and we sat down with a cup of tea.

This wonderful lady, who used her skills to help others, had a problem herself. She could not conceive and, although no medical fault had been found, her husband, also a doctor, and herself had been trying unsuccessfully for seven years. She wondered if I could help.

I told her I couldn't guarantee anything, but we would try some healing. A few months later she telephoned; she was pregnant. During her visit, my guide had told her that she would have two children. Heaven has since blessed her with the second.

It was 1985, and Angela brought her son, Tony, an autistic child, for healing. I didn't know how I was going to deal with this child. He was everywhere: in the kitchen eating cornflakes and jam, throwing everything all over the place, his mother and father apologising.

I gently took his hand, and he followed me into the room and sat down. He didn't move throughout his healing. His parents were amazed; they hadn't ever seen him sit so still. My guide said I needed to see him again, and I decided to call in Bill, the gentleman whose brother had communicated in 1978. I had heard that Bill was using colour in healing and I felt this might be beneficial to Tony.

Bill arrived at my home and, as we set up the coloured bulbs, he told me of how he had made his trip to Paris, where his brother's remains were.

I was astounded. "How did you know where to go, Bill?" I asked.

"My brother gave me the information when he spoke through you. Don't you remember?"

I didn't, but I was so thrilled for him. True communication had brought a marvellous conclusion to Bill's story. The colour healing helped Tony and, some time later, his mother reported that he was not nearly as hyperactive as he had been in the past.

I started going out with Roy, a man I'd known for many years. He knew of my work, having had healing himself for a back problem some years before, which to date had never again troubled him. It seems that no back problem that has had healing has ever had a recurrence.

Roy and I married at Christmas 1986. I had told him then that my work was important to me and that I would never stop doing it, a fact which he accepted. He knows that, just as he goes about his daily work, I must go about mine, even though my hours are unsocial.

It was difficult for both of us during our first year together. Roy had always been a heavy drinker and I, too, found myself drinking a lot at weekends. Adapting again to marriage was not easy; I had become very independent and Roy had a mind of his own.

However, we reached a good balance. He no longer drinks at all and is helpful to me in my work. We spend all our spare time together; having coffee in our favourite cafe, sitting around in Broadstairs, a place which we both love; wandering around Charles Dickens' Bleak House, and generally watching the world go by for two days a week. Before we were married, I was working seven days a week.

We had just arrived home from Broadstairs one Sunday evening, when a loud knock on the door made me hasten to answer it. There stood Sarah, a lady in her mid-forties, breaking her heart. "I need to see you," she cried as I brought her in.

"There, there, love. Come in and sit down."

Roy went and made us a cup of tea while I gave her a cigarette and asked her to calm down. Then I saw him. The young lad standing beside her.

"She's my mam," he said.

This was why she was in such a state. I knelt down on the carpet, moved her hair from her tear-stained face and gently said, "He's all right, love, your son's all right."

"How do you know that?" she asked.

"I can see him, love."

Her son, George, had died suddenly from a heart attack. He had been only sixteen years old. I sat throughout the night with her, talking, smoking and drinking tea. Both she and I were glad she had come.

George was able to tell her he was with his father; this poor woman had lost her husband, then her son. Over the next year, I watched her return to the happy soul she had been before. She now knew she hadn't lost her two men; they'd just gone before.

Tommy, a local entertainer, phoned for an appointment, telling me he had been attending Spiritualist churches for twenty years. All that time, he had been searching for some information on a very personal matter.

"OK," I told him, "say nothing more, until I finish." Tommy switched on his tape recorder and, almost at once, his mother communicated. He sat there with not as much as a blink. His mother's name, she told me, was Agnes, but she was called Aggie.

She told him all he needed to know, right down to the fact that it was he who had found her dead. He was also given details of other people and, when his reading ended, I asked if he had any questions.

"You've answered everything," he said. "I've spent all these years searching for communication with my mother, walked in here, and you've provided everything in just one hour."

Tommy was more than pleased.

Toots arrived with a few friends for a reading, during which her brother communicated. She was so shocked when I exclaimed, "Eddy is here!"

He had passed two weeks before. She admitted she hadn't expected anything like this; her husband, John, not having any interest in such things, had sat outside in his car. Toots told me she would tell Doris, her sister-in-law, of her husband's return, but didn't feel Doris would come to see me herself because she was spending all of her time at church and was in a terrible state emotionally.

I asked Toots not to talk Doris into anything, but to let her decide for herself. However, a few days later, Doris made an appointment, as did her brother-in-law John.

Doris, when she arrived, was certainly in a traumatic state; she was suicidal. She and Eddy had only been married a year. She told me that she had mentioned to her vicar her intention to come and he had said, "Yes, I have heard of her," and went on to advise Doris not to even think about it.

"Well, no disrespect to your vicar, love, but, seeing the state you are in, I'm glad you have come."

The communication with her husband was marvellous. He even told her where his ashes were scattered and Eddy helped his wife to accept his survival.

John is now developing in one of my circles.

It was the Tuesday after the Bank Holiday when six ladies arrived for an appointment which had been made a few months before.

As one sat down, I could see her son put his arms around her shoulders; here was a sad lady. Her son had passed only the evening before on the Bank Holiday Monday, and one of the original six had given up her appointment for this lovely soul, who left my home elated.

Her son had been ill for just over a year, and she told me she had sat with him the day he died and told him he was going to a better place, where he would feel no more pain

Jenny had been to see me a year before, a fact I was unaware of for, dealing with so many people, I find it so difficult to remember faces. Of course, what discussion goes on between myself and a sitter is thrown from me as soon as I've finished, so I never know what anyone has been given. My guide, however, usually recalls the important facts. In Jenny's case, her man communicated; Reg had gone suddenly and was very emotional on his return. After the sitting, Jenny switched off her tape recorder and told me how, on her last visit, she had been told a separation was to occur between her and Reg; my guide had even given the exact weekend.

As the time drew near, she said that she thought my guide must be wrong, as they were so happy together and Chang Li had not been specific about the separation. Would it be through work, or through problems between them?

She didn't know, and Chang Li wouldn't say. However, at the beginning of that week, she suggested to Reg that they should visit relatives in Cornwall whom they hadn't seen for some time. They thoroughly enjoyed their time there but, on arriving home, Reg complained of indigestion and was obviously very tired after the long drive back.

Jenny woke up in the middle of the night to find Reg out of bed and in the bathroom. She called to him and, getting no reply, went to see if he was OK, finding him dead on the bathroom floor. He had suffered a heart attack.

She let me listen to Chang Li's tape from her previous visit. We then understood.

Jenny was feeling Reg's presence very strongly in the house, and I asked her to leave her tape recorder running when she went to bed. She did this and soon contacted me again, bringing the tape with her.

Reg's voice came through distinctly, calling his mother. I had heard of this happening before, but so far have been unable to find someone with sufficient knowledge of tapes to enable us to pick up the rest of Reg's conversation. Perhaps a reader of this book might have some advice to offer?

A few days after this sitting, I had news from Australia; my natural mother had died – for reasons known only to 'them upstairs.' I hadn't been meant to meet either of my parents – perhaps we will meet one day, somewhere in time.

Les came to me with emotional problems. His late wife spoke to him, and he was also told he would be marrying a lady quite a number of years younger than himself. He wouldn't accept this; however, the spirit side know best, and I attended their wedding in March of this year.

After his first sitting, Les brought his sister, Alice, to see me. Alice is a medium, a wonderful lady, and I was able to take them both on a journey through their childhood, back to their home, describing each room in detail. All sorts of evidence was poured out for them.

We all remain very close to this day. Alice even reads out Annie's poems at the Spiritualist churches where she takes services.

FOURTEEN

Roy had made a comment about how some people must think I never sleep, considering how the phone rings at all hours of the day and night. He once took a call from one of my students, seeking advice regarding his development.

When, after about an hour, I came off the telephone, I sat down with a cup of tea and heard my guide say, "Why don't you make a tape?"

"That's a jolly good idea, it certainly would give me some time if I did."

So, on Robbie Burn's birthday, I started my tape. I called it 'Psychic Development For Beginners', an easy step-by-step guide to mediumship, and I finished it in March. I found that, on advertising, requests poured in - not only from individuals, but from Spiritualist churches as well.

I have had wonderful letters from all over this country and the United States, from people who have begun groups using the tape, finding it most helpful.

I had to give up my work in the nursing home because the demands for readings and healings had grown so much. My work for spirit was, after all, my vocation and, of course, would have to come first at all times.

Furthermore, I was being invited as guest speaker to various meetings and functions, where I would talk about my work, answer questions as best I could and give a demonstration. I didn't mind these, as they were all for charitable causes, and I was pleased to be told at most of them that the attendances had shot up when it was found out that I would be guest for the evening.

Of course, there were always the sceptics; however, they are entitled to their opinion. I would never try to force my beliefs on anyone; I have the courage of my convictions. My path is wide, where others seem to be narrow.

Attending large public meetings, I always felt that the visiting medium should try to give a message to as many people as possible. After all, large numbers of people attending these meetings all hoped for a personal contact from a loved one, and I always left feeling rather sorry that only five or six out of a few hundred could receive something.

Of course, there was nothing I could do about it. I had my orders: "You must always work alone," and I was certainly not criticising these wonderful people who were dedicated to their work. I, personally, didn't feel I could do it; I'd die of fright in front of such an audience!

However, Chang Li had different ideas. On telling me to go and pick a vast area, I found myself very hesitant. However, on his insistence, I began making enquiries and, with Roy's help, managed to contact the Manager of Margate Football Stadium.

I was uncertain of being allowed to hire the place once it was known what I wanted it for. The Manager had given me an appointment to discuss the matter and, not at all hopeful, we went along.

"What do you want the football ground for?" he said.

Well, here goes. "I want to hold a psychic evening."

"Oh, you mean a seminar?" he said.

"Yes, something like that."

After chatting for about half an hour, I won him over. I couldn't take it in for a while: I'd actually secured Margate Football Stadium.

I went to see Tommy, the entertainer mentioned earlier, and asked if he would consider helping me by entertaining during the evening. He readily agreed and, with the help of Tommy and his wife, we had tickets printed, made out posters, and began spreading the word.

While I was lying in bed one evening, reading DJ Ray Moore's life story, Doris Stokes appeared in front of me and told me to get in touch with Derek Jameson. "He'll help you," she said.

I already knew that Doris loved this man and his wife so, without hesitation, I put pen to paper asking Derek if he would send me a letter of encouragement. That was all I would need.

As the time drew near I was very nervous. What if I don't get anything? What if no one shows up? All sorts of questions, and all completely negative.

When I answered the telephone one morning, with pen in hand and appointment book ready as usual, the lady asked for me.

"Speaking," I replied.

"Ellen Jameson here."

"Yes," I answered turning to my next available appointment. As she spoke, the penny dropped; it was Derek's wife! He had told her that anyone booking a football stadium to get her message across, had to be worth talking to, and he wanted me to be a guest on his chat show. I didn't even know he had a chat show!

When I told Annie about it, she said, "It must be his TV show."

"I didn't even know he did one."

"Yes, on Sky," she informed me.

Of course, I didn't have Sky and I never watched television anyway, as I just didn't get the time.

So it was we arrived at the film studios, and I couldn't believe how calm I was. I met Derek in make-up and he introduced me to his wife Ellen. He was much taller than I imagined and Ellen looked a timid little soul, but I could see such strength of character in her. I knew why he looked so happy: he was a lucky man.

Derek was very kind, as was everyone I met at the studios. We had a wonderful day, and he didn't only give me encouragement. I was going to take it as it came. Spirit side had never let me down before, and they certainly weren't going to now!

I had put my ads in the papers; the last one would be in the Psychic News on the Saturday, two days before the event.

On the morning of my big night, tickets had been sold out. We went to the stadium, where Tommy set up his sound equipment and arranged the seating. It did look nice, the stage surrounded with baskets of flowers which I was going to give to recipients of messages that evening.

I had given Annie ten envelopes to give to ten people before I arrived; she was to ask each of them to put an object belonging to them into the envelope and leave it on stage. I would start by demonstrating psychometry (the reading of an object), after which we would have an interval; then I would open up and allow as many spirit visitors in as was possible.

Roy went off to pick up neighbours who hadn't transport and take them to the stadium. The telephone never stopped ringing with good luck messages.

I had told Roy I mustn't arrive until five minutes before I was due to start, so that I wouldn't be able to get into any conversation with anyone. This was so that no one could say I was talking to someone who could, perhaps, be passing me information.

When we drove up, there was not a parking space to be found and people unable to get a ticket had queued up in the hope of getting in. With the permission of the manager, they were allowed in, a hundred more than there should have been. The stadium was overcrowded.

I had specifically asked for the bar to be opened, to allow anyone to have a drink if they so wished. Smoking was also permitted. This was to be a laid-back evening, after which we would have a dance and a sing-song.

I took the envelopes willy-nilly and read each object before asking who the owner was. All ten were amazed at the accuracy.

From one envelope, I took out a set of car keys and described the lady I saw using these keys. Took her into her sitting-room, describing her new three piece suite and her dog lying by the fire.

On asking for the owner of the keys to step forward, great applause rang out as the lady I'd described came to collect them. She confirmed the accuracy of all that I'd said and seen. Later on, she had to be told to be quiet as she couldn't get over it! Most amusing.

A ring which I read led me to talk about a baby, which would be soon arriving from spirit side to the ring's owner. When this lady stepped forward, we could all see she was expecting.

A strange-looking object I was reading reminded me of a face one would see on a totem pole. Its owner, I revealed, was very psychic and worked in healing for spirit. After other details were given, I asked this person to collect his object; out of the crowd walked Bill, my friend and healer, who had helped me with Tony, the autistic child. I almost cried with joy, as I hadn't seen Bill since we did the colour healing together.

Tommy had everyone singing and clapping their hands. He had been desperate to develop his gifts for a long time. I told him he had one great gift, and that was in bringing pleasure to people through his singing and guitar playing. A wonderful guy whom we love dearly, and without whose help the evening wouldn't have gone as it did.

The second half found me going into the audience.

A brother, who had been electrocuted after climbing up a pylon, communicated with his sister and his aunt.

A wife who returned to her first husband. This communication caused uproar, as his second wife who was with him had never been told he'd been married before. Of course, he had to admit it before they went home!

A gentleman returning, having only been on the spirit side one week, after a major motorway accident.

I found out later that this gentleman had been coming to see me. Death had not stopped him!

All in all, twenty-six people received communication; I had been on-stage for four hours. It was a wonderful evening. Roy was marvellous and videoed it all.

I found that people had travelled from all over the country to be there; even some from America had secured tickets prior to their arrival in the United Kingdom. Coaches were driven from Spiritualist churches in various parts of the country. The spirit side hadn't let anyone down. Of course, this event created more interest and I did more work, to add to my already overloaded schedule.

A gentleman caller made an appointment for two and told me he couldn't give the names, but I would recognize the people when I saw them and would I go to an address a few hours drive away, on a certain date, to see them?

I apologized, and told the gentleman that because so many people had made bookings months before, it would not be possible for me to travel. He rang me back to confirm their appointment and said that they would come to me. I cannot, however, disclose their identities.

Asking Chang Li his reasons for me having to do a public demonstration, he told me that time would bring the required result; the seed had been planted in a new field.

I accepted his reply without further question. Many, many people have asked when I will be doing another one - I cannot answer that; I take my instructions from spirit.

The taking of any form of drugs had also become an important issue – having stopped them myself some time ago. Chang Li stresses the need for us to use a clear mind; pills and drugs damage the spirit. So I do try to get this message across.

During discussions, many people have mentioned how, when they were young, they would speak to unseen people; of course, I fully understand. I tell them children are psychic and should be encouraged. It is, however, very difficult for people to move out of the mould and, all too often, their psychic gifts are suppressed.

Almost every day we read in the papers of people having premonitions; sadly, usually reported after the event.

Can man control his destiny?

With the power of the mind he can. It can be used towards a better understanding of each other. On the other hand, using it wrongly will destroy us.

In his wisdom, Chang Li had told me that insight is a direct transmission with no need of Scriptures, or the teaching of any Doctrine, but an immediate communication from mind to mind.

We humans suffer through materialism. The more we gather, the happier we seem to be. All things temporary have become important. We are losing ourselves, fighting against change to please ourselves and not our souls. This cannot be. Life here is temporary, as are all material things, so there is a great need for reality in our lives. When we stop thinking of ourselves and more of others, only then will spirituality overcome materialism.

Meditation is all-important for reality, thus bringing

compassion and awareness to the individual soul. Death is no escape, as we have to abide by Karmic laws, the laws of cause and effect. As in the words of the Bible 'What does it profit a man to gain the whole world and suffer the loss of his own soul?' A true interpretation of reality.

It is good to see more and more young people searching for answers, knowing that there is more to life than life itself seems to offer.

I try to answer all questions asked of me as best I can, but I, too, have a long way to go. Each day is a new day of learning for me. I will continue to teach, to learn and to communicate for the benefit of others and of my own soul.

I, too, am only human, and the gift is not for me.

ANNIE'S POEMS

*Below, and on the following pages
is a collection of
Ann Hewitt's poems,
sent from the Spirit side*

When you feel you are alone, remember it's not true,
Because I'm always here beside you in everything you do.
So when you feel you've had enough, that you've been
        pushed too far,
Don't despair, for I am there, no matter where you are.

☆

As I sit and wonder, of what to do that's right,
I wonder of the dreams I have, that come to me at night.
I cannot recall them, the day sends them away,
But surely they are dreams I had, of what to do today.

☆

On this earth are many things, events and daily happenings,
That we don't know the answer to, like Why and When
        and How and Who.
But someone somewhere had the gift, to tell us what we
        want to know,
So if the answer's somewhere, seek and you'll get what
        you want to know.

☆

When the pen is heavy to hold, do not give in but
    just behold,
The words as they are written, are warm, are worth their
    weight in gold.
For you a chosen one and they are very few, so write on
    with your pen and see,
That this was meant for you.

☆

On a hill somewhere, sometime ago, stood the greatest
    friend of mine,
Sunshine all around the place, lit up the beauty of his face.
Were you a non-believer be, he stood there for you and me.
The greatest man there ever was, the purest psychic
    Son of God.
Somewhere there's a garden that you and I can't see,
Where all the lovely people sit, loved ones of you and me.
It really is a picture, it needs no rain or sun.
Because it used love to grow, the flowers everyone.
So when the days are ending, of ones we hold so dear,
There is no need to be afraid, the picture's very clear.
Of roses, trees and flowers, so lovely to behold,
And meet up with our loved ones, we once again can hold.
On the other side is sunshine and very little rain,
On the other side is happiness and never any pain.
So when you lose somebody, even though you grieve,
They are better off than us, they chose their time to leave.
He saw that they were needed, to carry on the work,
That happens on the other side.
They tell us when they talk, of what a lovely place it is,
No worries cares or woes, so though you grieve, don't do
    for long,
When a loved one goes.

☆

Friends can help to ease a pain, friends can make you
    smile again
And even when it's hard and rough, the going getting yet
    more tough.
A friend can make it all worthwhile, a friend can help you
    cross the stile.
That because you've been a friend to them,
They'll help you when you need a friend.

☆

Don't wait around for things to come, sometimes you have
    to go alone,
To meet your future with a smile.
Though you're not happy all the while,
It's no good sitting back to wait,
For chances, just anticipate,
Then you can go ahead and win,
Not just today but everything
Will come to you if you just try,
Above all smile.

☆

Knowing that you're needed to help to ease a load,
Can make your life seem easier and see a clearer road
Or fortunes that may lay ahead.
So don't just give up hope,
But concentrate on what is good.
Don't ever feel alone.
For there is someone somewhere to help along the way,
To watch over your shoulder and help you ease that load
And you will never stumble
On the rough and rugged road.

☆

There is someone somewhere who guides this pen for me,
To write down the things I do, are alien to me.
So who are you? You're welcome,
I'm glad to know you're there,
So guide my pen for longer,
These poems I can share.

☆

Somewhere there's a baby crying,
Somewhere there is someone dying,
Somewhere there are dogs of war,
Not knowing what they're fighting for.
I cannot stop it happening,
I only wish I could,
But I am on the other side,
Where everything is good.

☆

In the corners of my mind are memories not too
    hard to find,
Of all the things we used to do, when you were here just
    we two.
I had to share you then most times, I didn't like it much.
But at the end of all it is, the two of us still close in touch.

☆